# Listen Mama

# Listen Mama

**M.S.P. Williams**

First paperback edition January 2021

Edited by BuzBooks

Book design by BuzBooks

ISBN (Paperback) 978-0-578-73017-2
ISBN (eBook) 978-0-578-73016-5
ISBN (Hardcover) 978-0-578-73130-8

mspwilliams.com

twitter.com/msp_williams

instagram.com/msp_williams

facebook.com/williams.msp

*Dedicated with Unconditional Love to Selita, Mama Dear,
Stephanie, Dominique, Dante, Cheyenne, Jamon, Little Greg,
Janet, Michelle, and every woman, man, and child in the
world, trying their very best, day after day . . .*

# AUTHOR'S NOTE

The events and conversations in this book have been set down to the best of the author's ability and memory, although some names and details have been changed to protect the privacy of certain individuals.

*For the first time, Mama, my soul will rest in peace. Hopeful, because it seems, that you could be what you once were, and might forever remain—happy—in more than my dreams . . .*

*May 24, 1993*

*I had my reconstructive surgery this morning. It hurt so bad Mama. I have been sleeping most of the day due to the pain pills, but if it helps take away my burns and scars so I don't get made fun of as much, it will be worth it. Not to mention getting punched and kicked, and stuff. When I was beat up the last time in March that was it for me, and made me decide to go ahead with this, even though I was really scared. My cover story I told Mama Dear about the bruises was that I finally got to play football with the other boys that day, and it just got a bit rough. She seemed to accept it, but after seeing all my cousins grow up, and being a nurse, I think she was just too kind to tell me she knew what really happened.*

*Love you very much. And don't worry about not being there when I woke up. I know you would if you could.*

*Oh, and my 14th birthday is today also. If you could have been there that it would be great. But it's totally ok and I understand, because I know that you are in the hospital too. Only it's a different kind of hospital for different kind of help. You never sleep hardly, you have been hearing voices through the tv telling you "secrets" about people around you, and you claimed Cheyenne's dad was not Ray, but actually some local radio DJ that you had met on his Army leave? Yelling, cursing, just, it's all too much . . . You need rest and medical attention, and have some problems that our love just can't fix . . . However, once they actually admitted you into the clinic, you were on your best behavior. Because of this, and your refusal to take medication, the clinic could only hold you for a seventy-two-hour observation period. One nurse told me that if you didn't 'wig out' in front of them, this was the best their facility could offer. I can't wait to welcome you home tomorrow.*

*Now although you screamed to the heavens that everyone was against you, that's just not the case Mama. The vote to have you committed was a lot closer than you would have ever imagined. In fact, I'm fairly certain that more people than not were against you being sent, including Olivia and her kids, June Bug, and perhaps Lynell. I followed the lead of Mama Dear (as always) along with Janet and Rosalind, and did not object. But the concerns of the rest of the family had me pretty worried. They said they did not know what might happen to you, that this was wrong, and nobody's freedom should be taken away from them. And I'll be honest, I was really scared due to the portrayal of mental institutions in films and television. For all I knew they would have you locked up on the same wing as some psychopath or deranged killer . . .*

*I was mainly terrified at the potential for abuse and mistreatment at the hands of the clinic's staff. For one, I thought it was more like a jail scenario, with all degrees of the mentally ill lumped together. And two, I had not too long ago caught the Frances Farmer movie about her life and was horrified at how she was treated. However, when I visited you yesterday, I was relieved to see it was not like that all. The hospital was clean and well furnished. Although I arrived with people you consider "conspirators", you still spoke to me and no one else. During our talk you kept moving around, and only later did Rosalind point out that it was due to a nurse shadowing you to see how you interacted with your family. You didn't want to talk too long, and I get it. And again, I'm sorry. We just all want you to feel better.*

But I'm not all the way sure I will be there to see that. I tried to kill myself this morning before my surgery. There was No tear-riddled notes, no haunting/cryptic phone calls to family members either. So how did it get to that point, you ask? I had just come back from the pre-surgery doctor's appointment. We fought about something as well, I think you threw out a classic, "Maybe you should've just never been born" line, so that didn't really help move the conversation forward... And I was complaining about not wanting to go to school after the appointment, and argued I should stay home due to how the kids there treat me. And you said, "That's what happens to people that don't stand up for themselves."

Mostly, I just decided that it was time. Time to put an end to the string of misfortune others would merely describe as 'growing pains.' Time to quit facing the stares, the taunts. Time to stop letting others make me feel bad for something that I had no control over. Just as they had no input over whether they grew up to be tall, good looking, rich, or what have you. The only argument against not going through with it would be that it would have made Mama Dear sad. But that was no longer enough . . .

I was extremely curious over what would have happened. For instance, where would I go? Now, one would naturally think heaven, right? Seeing as how I had not done anything unbelievably wrong up to this point of my life. And though I vaguely recalled hearing that Catholics could not get into heaven if they committed suicide, I figured this wouldn't apply to me since I hardly ever went to church anyway. I was basically playing the odds. I mean, what were the chances of the afterlife being as crummy as the present life? Of course, I'd miss Mama Dear, but since she always wanted the best for me, I was sure she'd come to understand my actions. And, I was really banking on seeing her up there one day. Me and Granny up in heaven, watching soap operas during the day, while I hooped with the angels at night. Everyone else? Well, I'd see them as soon as they got there. If they ever got there . . . The way I saw it, if you saw someone you knew, then you'd recognize them through their spirit, if you will. And *you'd remember all the good times you'd had together, and so on. However, if you did not see a person you knew from your past, you'd never miss them. How could you? There would be too much heavenly joy popping off all around you.*

*The house was unusually empty, and I decided to seize the day. I took one of your many pistols, this one being an old 38 special you had taken from Mama's house (and blamed me for, no less), and I locked myself in my room. I turned on my record player, put on the only record I had, George Michael's "One More Try", and sat on the edge of the bed, waited for the last verse to end, put the gun to my temple, and pulled the trigger. What happened? Why am I still here? Well, it just clicked—without the Boom. I was like hmm, what a buzzkill (pun absolutely intended). I figured out how to open the chamber, and I looked inside. Six chambers, four bullets, and I got one of the empty two. What are the odds? Well of course the odds are 33 percent that I would luck up, but I mean, the cosmic odds? And even though I knew my chances of success went up prodigiously with each successive pull of the trigger, I kind of felt the moment had passed, and I decided to leave well enough alone, and went to watch He-Man. I mean, priorities, right?*

*I promised myself that there would be no more attempts (yeah probably a lie). You know, there are just some things in this world that you can never get past . . . Instances that forever mark you—on the inside or out— that are inescapable. No matter how far you run, no matter how loud you scream. We learned about an author in English class, Primo Levi, who was a Holocaust survivor. He survived the horrors, and eventually became a big-time writer and chemist. Yet even after all of this, he chose to end his own life, forty plus years after being liberated from Auschwitz. But it seems as if he only gained freedom in name only, because his mind and his soul were still being tortured all those decades later.*

*My classmates were shocked: "Why? How could he, especially after surviving that tragedy?" Well, I wasn't puzzled at all. The short answer is that he never in fact 'survived' that tragedy to begin with. We don't surrender our experiences once we are out of the moment. Or somehow magically transcend the pain. He merely sidestepped and bided time until an inevitable dark end he'd be holding off for far too long. Forged a great career, had a wife and children, but the internal horror remained . . . If someone went through the same thing, became a junkie, and then killed themselves, would there be a ton of questions surrounding him? In this author's case, the pain took the roundabout way, yet still caught up with him in the end.*

*Still looking for my place in the sun . . .*

*- Manny*

*P.S.*
*Thank you for this journal very much. Sorry for the long letter. I just really like writing in it, and hope you read it someday. It's one of the best presents I have ever gotten and I really appreciate it.*

*June 16, 1993*

*I went to the doctor and he decided I was able to return back to school. I also started my injections last week. It has been crazy to say the least. The same kids who used to avoid me like the plague were now all up under me, asking about my surgery, being on television, and things of that nature. My head is filled with silicone twice a week, and these injections aren't that painful, all in all. They would best be described as vaccine shots in your head instead of your arm. However, the first few hours afterwards were tough due to headaches. This would have to be from the extra weight and tension on my head from the fluid building up over time while the skin was being stretched farther and farther. Not avoidable though, because they need more skin to then cut and sew over my burned skin. Like something out of a science fiction movie. At school, to hide the bumps from sticking out in my head, I wear a two-tone brown and white ski cap. Keep in mind this is during the spring/summer Texas heat and humidity, and will go on for two straight months. I get plenty of stares for my fashion choices—even from you. But from a guy who's used to stares, it's really no big deal.*

*- Manny*

*July 26, 1993*

*Kids can be so cruel. Scratch that. Kids can be Downright Evil. I'm talking spiteful, vengeful, mean-spirited, and deplorable. I think that covers it. And I hate to throw a loud, big time 'pity-party' so close to the last one, but Stephanie got picked on at summer school today. Somebody on the bus said she lived in a 'raggedy' house. She took exception, and they went at it. The other kid is two years older, but Steph didn't come out of it with a scratch on her.*

*That's my girl. Well, actually she's not, because we fight like cats and dogs over everything from what to watch on TV ("Arsenio Hall" vs. "Three's Company" reruns) to who gets the last popsicle. But I am super proud of her because I never would have reacted that way. When I get the business from bullies—the punches, taunts and threats, the name-calling, stares, mean jokes (Scarface/Freddy Kruger), I never fought back. Never! Oh, I wince and whimper and sulk and make ugly faces of my own, but I have never once fought back. And I hate myself for it.*

*I just did not, and still do not get it. I can see wanting to beat up the snobby, rich kid. Or the jerk that trips you in the hallway. They actually deserve it. But picking on a poor, disfigured kid—what the heck is that? Oh yeah, I don't constantly realize that I'm overweight and horribly scarred, so why not reinforce it by kicking my butt every day. That'll make me learn.*

*Mama Dear, as usual, is the hero in all of this. She wrote a letter to Marvin Zindler at Channel 13 Eye Witness News. You remember him, right? He's our nationally known human-interest reporter who does everything from taking doctors to third-world countries to giving assistance to the poor, to reporting on Houston restaurants with "Slime in the ice machine!" (and while delivering this catchy jingle, he was adorned in a pimped-out buttercream suit with matching Stetson hat and boot combo, no less). He even made a movie with Burt Reynolds and Dolly Parton that was pretty funny. A man of many talents.*

*An interesting side note, as a teen, Mama Dear was a seamstress at this reporter's family's store, Zindler's. When he came to interview me, he seemed to genuinely remember her. I told my story, and I sang my song, and that was it. I got a spot on the six o'clock local news. I listened to Zindler's talk of my horrible accident, the cruelty of my peers, da, da, da . . . In the end, he hooked me up with Dr. Joseph Agris, a great plastic surgeon who has helped countless children.*

*I had my second surgery a last week and it was by far worse. I mean, we're talking pain upon pain here. Unbearable, Greek mythology-style torment. And I knew this going in. But being forewarned and being cut the heck up are two entirely different things. However, there was a medical student (on his surgery rotation, I believe), who was very friendly in the operating room. He even played me PM Dawn's "I'd Die Without You" as I underwent anesthesia. Another good guy whose name I have misplaced in the Book of Life . . .*

*When I awoke after surgery, I had no idea where, or who, I was. I couldn't speak, and my throat felt as if it had hot embers running through it. I could barely see, and only later would find out my eyes and face were extremely swollen—side effects of the surgery I was then unaware of. My next joy would be today when it came time to remove the stitches from my* head. I mean, they were literally cutting them out of my head with scissors, while I was wide awake, without any of that pesky little anesthesia! Then, there were the inserts the doctor put in my head. I can only describe them as being extremely odd and uncomfortable. Imagine three tennis ball-sized, liquid-filled implants in your head, poking out for all to see. And my biggest fear, which my cousin DJ played upon, was that if I talked any smack to him, he would throw darts at me and pop them open. Nice imagery, I know.

I had my second surgery yesterday, two weeks before I began high school. I complained so much the first time around to Mama Dear that she called the hospital and had them place a morphine drip in my room. It releases a measured amount of medication in intervals that have been predetermined by the doctor. It goes directly into your blood stream, which is much quicker than digesting a tablet. However, I was under the impression that every time I pressed the release button, I would be receiving a dose of medicine, so I was just hitting the button with the abandon of a Jeopardy superstar. And though I know better now, at the time, I swore it actually did give me more than the nurse claimed. And though I've never done drugs in my life, if I did, it would be something in the opiate family, because quite frankly, morphine rocks.

On a serious note, what has helped me soldier on through the recovery process was flipping through the before-and-after portfolio Dr. Agris had in his lobby. There was one photo of an eight or nine-year-old girl who had the same procedure done as me. Her hair became entangled in a go-cart after it flipped over. She had beautiful long dark brown hair, and almost all of it had been ripped out—along with a good portion of her scalp. The doc said she took it like a champ—no tantrums, no protests. I decided to do my best to follow her lead.

Janet did some great research on my accident for the subsequent lawsuit that followed. I found it not too long ago when Mama Dear had me help her clean out her filing cabinet. Among the highlights are that the IV infiltrated because they basically messed up the composition of the *solution. I also discovered that the trauma that ensued went down in less than five minutes. That's approximately how long it took for all my burns to occur. So, in theory, if someone had checked in on me in say two minutes, then maybe my injuries would only have been half as bad. And that kind of hurts, knowing that it didn't have to be this way . . .*

*The real kicker, however, came from reading the depositions that were taken among our family, the hospital staff, and lawyers. I know the name of the doctor who messed me over. He took no blame whatsoever. He told you that, "Well, he could be dead." I know his name, and I know where he currently practices. And I mention this only because I truly feel that one day that he will apologize to me and take his overdue portion of the blame. In fact, I'm certain of it. I have to be, for my own peace of mind.*

*After the healing process plays itself out, I really think my head will be greatly improved. Even now thought my hair is matted down, and my scalp is caked with scars, it looks Much Better. Now, I'm sure others might find this hard to believe due to the scars I have left on my forehead and my surgery incision which cannot be changed, but they'd just have to take my word on it if they didn't know me beforehand.*

*Every now and then, when I catch someone staring just a little too long at me—with that certain mixture of curiosity and repulsion over my state of appearance—I feel it's my duty to soothe them. To let them know that yes, I've had a rough go of it, but who really hasn't? And no, contrary to their better judgment, I am a reasonably happy and well-adjusted person, all in all. And no, I don't care about people asking me about my head after all these years; I've come to expect, and accept it. I guess I finally learned to fight back a little bit, just like Steph. And besides, these rude people have no clue that my biggest scars are on the inside . . .*

*- Manny*

*August 16, 1993*

*Today was the first day of high school. Not too many friendly faces. The kids dress a lot differently than they did last year in 8ᵗʰ grade. It used to be buttoned down shirts were a big deal. Now they are wearing tee shirts with like cartoons on them, sweatshirts, and some jeans that are ridiculously huge and falling down sometimes. And then there's me with my blue silk Hawaiian shirt and skin tight black slacks. Yeah, once an outcast, always an outcast. I will make the proper adjustments and come back to war tomorrow. I saw two kids that were at my old middle school in Aldine before I transferred. They are twins Rodney and Ronald. Nerdy, but good guys. Love basketball like me, and the show Martin. Will try to catch up to them one day and see how they have been the last year or two.*

*- Manny*

*November 19, 1993*

*In English class today, out of nowhere whatsoever, a deep-thinking class-mate named Eric said, "The circumference of your perception, helps deter-mine the diameter of your reality." Now I have no idea what that means, but I swore to myself as soon as he said it that I would repeat it to every-one till I found someone who either understood, or convinced me it was nonsense. I heard his uncle (or cousin?) is Mookie Blaylock the basketball star. He himself is tall and can play too, so it seems to track. I saw a year or so ago on NBA Inside Stuff that Pearl Jam actually named their band after him because they were such huge basketball fans, but then changed it, because, you can't just take someone's name. Small world. On a side note, Hunger Strike, the song Pearl Jam members did with Chris Cornell is Magnificent.*

*- Manny*

*January 1, 1994*

*Well, the New Year started off with Fireworks today, but not the good kind. You have been acting funny for a long time again, and I think the family is going to put you back in the hospital. You've been hearing things, thinking people were following you, carrying around two and three guns, and just last night making us sleep in closets so that 'hit men' would not kill us in our beds at night. When this happened last year, I just thought it was stress, that's what everyone in the family said. Maybe post-partum depression, which I hear women can get after having multiple babies in a short time. You have had 3 in 3 ½ years . . . Or that maybe you just had a drinking or drug problem. Uncle June Bug says some crazy stuff too when he is drunk or high. And to be real, that would be so much easier to handle. A real, concrete problem to send you to rehab for, and yell at you about. But this, this is so much worse. Because you can't be yelled at or blamed for this. Because of not knowing how to help you, or what we, or you, are fighting in your mind. And it's a battle you are losing more and more each day. And maybe that makes me a monster—but at least it makes me and honest monster . . .*

*- Manny*

*February 5, 1994*

*School is the same old same old. Classes are harder, kids are bigger. But I am holding my own. I have a few guys that I talk to a bit. I am considered the "funny/crazy" one in the group because of some of the outlandish stories I tell. If they only know how crazy I really was . . . It's a magnet school, so kids come from all over to attend. There's a pretty big mix of races here, and some from backgrounds and countries I had never even seen or heard of before: United Arab Emirates, San Salvador, you name it. I keep my head down mostly and stick to my work. The competition is fierce. They run stats for GPA for each class, and will give us rankings at the end of each year. There is already talk of PSAT's, extracurricular activities, internships, and summer jobs. Some of these kids have a Plan. I mean a Life Plan like kids you see on tv shows. They will intern with this company, that has a relationship with this school, that will lead to this future job followed by grad school and then the next big job. Whereas I am happy to make it through the next math quiz coming up and not missing the Metro Bus because it comes so close to the bell. I will ease into it and not try to overwhelm myself, which would be the ultimate recipe for disaster. But I can't help feeling that I was just born behind, in comparison to everyone else . . .*

*May 24, 1994*

*A new entry for the 'craziest birthday's ever' files today. German Chocolate cake was delicious. Sizzler was as good as ever. But have to talk about the skating rink thing that happened and the kid you saved today! He had a seizure I guess, and just collapsed on the floor. There were so many people there, and no one, I mean no one did anything but you. Some screamed, and cried and yelled for help – but you came running in there and did something. You cleared his mouth from the vomit, put a belt in there so he wouldn't bite his tongue, had the manager call an ambulance . . . Wow, where did you even learn to do that stuff, from tv? I know you went to school to be a speech patholo-gist but was not aware you had skills like that. Maybe you should try to find a job as an EMT or paramedic, because I think you would be great.*

*Love you very much, and so proud to be your son more than ever.*

*- Manny*

*December 18, 1994*

*I am deep into my sophomore year of high school, and I finally made what I consider a true close friend who is two grades above me, and happens to suffer from bipolar disorder as well just like you. The general feeling was that she just was a lazy child, never had much going for her, and would never amount to anything. She was moody, insolent, sarcastic—you name something bad, and she was called it. But she was also funny, smart, a great writer (inspired me to start writing poetry), a good cook, a great dancer, a good listener, and many more positives. She told me that several times in the last few years she was put in a mental hospital, doped up, the whole nine yards. On Lithium, I believe. Same thang Mr. Cobain wrote about. Upon hearing this, I felt so bad for all the times me and others at school had talked bad about her —you know, going along with the crowd on her minimal self-worth, etc.*

*People tell me things, Mama, and I'm just not sure why. I think it's proven worldwide that I'm much more of an expert at talking as opposed to listening—yet they still line up. Maybe I throw them off guard by relating and speaking to them on any number of subjects, and they feel a false sense of security in opening up to me? I'm not sure. I'm not smart like an orthodontist to make that type of judgment call. They talk, and I listen— or pretend to. Somebody one said that, "Most people don't really listen to you, instead of just waiting for their turn to speak?" Well, that would be me. It's not to be rude or disrespectful. It's just that I know way deep down that nothing they say that day will be half as interesting or clever as what I plan on rolling out in the next minute. I race through jokes/stories/puns in my mind to put on a show for all I know, and I never bother with what's coming through on the other end of the line. Not because I need to entertain, but because I have to. I want them walking away thinking, "Man, he may be shady, but he sure can tell a hell of a story!"*

*It helps me work through my day. Most of the time, that is. Because every now and then, even the great Manny is caught off guard and must take heed to what the other person is telling me. Yet again, even when I do submit to their pleas to hear their life stories, I still wonder, why me? Do I know them that well? Or is it they think they know me well enough to take this step? Or maybe they can easily look at my face and tell I have danced with devil for a song or two, so I may be a little more apt to relate to their life-shattering pain than Kirsten at the country club? Or maybe they just figure odds are that I probably don't have any friends or a girl to run and tell their secrets to, so it will be safe to store them with me.*

*Well, one girl I barely knew came out to me at lunch that she was a kleptomaniac who liked to steal socks. Yeah, this was during burgers at McDonald's, so it's not because I tried to put any 'moves' on her. Another told me how her mom had her locked away for stealing from her, and after juvie didn't work, her mom trumped up charges to get her sent to Cypress Creek Mental Facility. Another dude told me how he was hooked on meth since leaving the Army (lied about his age and signed up at 17), had flings with a ton of girls, but was too scared to take an AIDS test, and had more than a few warrants out on him. This dude concerns me. Because 1, Why and How are you still in high school if you are a meth addicted army reject. And 2, we had just met on the basketball court about twenty minutes prior . . .*

*But I don't look down on them, especially the biggie secrets. I'm talking the kind that stop you from shutting your eyes and keep you up at 2:00 a.m. wondering, "Why did I have to learn this today?" The kind that keeps one from shrieking like the rest of an audience at a horror film, because that silent person in the crowd has seen true misery in their life— and nothing on that screen can come close to replicating it. These people give me their secrets, and I would love to give them right back. They tell me things I have no right to know.*

*The dirty little secret of the world, is that bad things happen to good people. All the time. Our political and spiritual leaders like to gloss over in their lectures and sermons on how, "If you do your part as a good American/Christian/child, the world can/will be yours someday." They have to keep the sad facts hidden or else everyone will see the randomness in their wins and losses in life, and perhaps say screw it and be terrible all the time. If people realize they have just as many odds of being rewarded for it as they do being punished while being pious, where would we be? As a society, we just can't have that, now can we?*

*And I say that wordy intro to tell you of the sad story of a good girl, who definitely did not deserve what befell upon her in life. She's the same girl I told you earlier was moody and distant, looked down upon by her family during childhood. Very disrespectful to their authority over her. Well, you want to know why? Because she was molested by a close relative from the time she was five until the age of thirteen. And some of those family members knew. But they dismissed it. Called her a liar. And worse, the ones who thought there could have been veracity to her claims immediately* took the position that she had brought it on herself by always being 'up under' him, and other grown men. Yeah, a five-year-old is really 'asking for it,' you heartless monsters. In my mind's eye, once going through something of that nature, you basically have license to do whatever you want to in life, as long as you don't hurt innocent others. Want to drink—well, be my guest. Take drugs to numb the pain—knock yourself out. Mope around in black and listen to depressing music while cursing out your elders—hey, rock on. To paraphrase some singer whose name I forget, "At the end of the day, who's really to say what's wrong with being sad?"

She told me that she was thinking over, and over, about 'it.' That 'it' weighed on her mind, her body, and her soul. She couldn't even give "it" a name, that's how scary this monster was from her childhood. The great Stephen King couldn't have conjured up anything more terrifying. She said she couldn't speak on the subject—because her words would quickly turn to screams. But she did talk, in an urgent and rapid manner, as if she'd lose her courage if she slowed down for an instant to catch a breath that would not ease her anyway. And she was pretty difficult to understand at times, with the intermittent sobs and yells punctuating her tale, but I more than got the gist of it.

When she built up the nerve to first tell her relatives at age ten about what was happening, the kinder ones responded, "Oh, we didn't know. You should have said something sooner." This was their reply to a little girl that had walked alone through the valley of death to finally ask for help. And then it kept happening for three more years. What about hugging her, getting her some therapy, getting him locked the hell up and/or killed? All seem pretty reasonable responses to me, but maybe I'm the crazy one? She said it stopped suddenly at age thirteen out of nowhere. I'm thinking maybe he was scared she was old enough to get pregnant, and there would be living, breathing evidence of his crimes. And shortly thereafter she asked 'it' why he had done such horrendous things to her. His response was, "It was done to me as a child too, so I did it to you."

*At the end of our talk that day, she seemed to find whatever little shred of peace I tried to empower her with. She thanked me, with a smile, tears streaming down her face. She's trying to make something out of herself and here she is thanking me for just listening to her, something that should be a God-given right, and not a privilege or reward. Well, I had to thank her. For trusting me with a burden I was not sure I even wanted to attempt to carry. For living her life. For having the faith to keep on day after day, when most of us would have called it checkmate a long time ago. She was a hundred times stronger than I could ever be.*

*I left, and I went back home to watch the Incredible Hulk episode I had taped, with the saddest theme music in history made even more tragic given my state of mind. Then she called me. Not for another three-hour session, or to yell and scream at the heavens, but to tell me that she forgot to mention something really important before leaving. I asked her what. She said, "Manny, do you know what the worst part of it was?" I asked if she meant the physical part? "No," she replied. "The worst part was that he never said he was sorry. He never once even said he was sorry." And then I said that I was sorry, as if that might somehow help, her hearing the words from someone, and she started crying hysterically again, and I just listened, and I cried along with her.*

*- Manny*

*March 1, 1995*

*When I came home from school today, my grandmother, Mama Dear, was crying uncontrollably in the living room because my stepdad, Ray, had come by with the police and stolen my sister Cheyenne away. I'd never seen my grandmother cry before, and if God is Truly Good, I never will again. I knew Ray and you were having problems, and he is their father and all, but I never thought something like this would happen. I mean, you are back at your special hospital again getting trying to get better, for us, and to have you come home and see one of your kids missing . . . how cruel could he be? Divorce or not, how could he put that kind of pain on you? And Mama Dear? Being old and alone, and not having any idea what to do, she must have been so scared . . .*

*When I got home, Mama Dear asked me to cut Dante's hair, because I guess Ray said he would be back for his other two kids, Dominique and Dante, after they got back from school. She didn't want him to leave the house looking bad. Funny how Ray didn't mention coming back for me and Stephanie. I mean, he's our stepfather . . . but we're not really 'his kids,' so he doesn't really want us in this fight. I know it's selfish to say this, but that was one of the first things to come to my mind. I feel bad about that.*

*I really didn't want to cut Dante's hair, and not because it bothered me that I was asked, or that I was super busy; it's just that I was scared I would do a bad job. I haven't really got the whole blending thing down on my fades, and I didn't want to send Dante away with the old 'chili bowl' look! But I lucked up, and around 5:00 p.m., I cut it and it came out pretty good. Aunt Arleta told me so, and it made me smile.*

*But none of that matters, because at 7:00 p.m., Ray came back to Mama Dear's house with the police as promised. Mama Dear started crying again, and it broke my heart, but I wouldn't, I couldn't, show that to her. You told Dante and Dominique over the phone that they would get to go stay with their Daddy for a little while. Dante asked me if me and Steph would come and visit them. I told him, "Yeah, Poppa, you bet." And then I walked away so he wouldn't see me start to cry as well. I went to my room as I heard the cop car and Ray pull off, and then I felt free to cry my eyes out.*

*After the tears were finished, I wrote. And I wrote. And then I wrote some more. On how I would go to school and make money to get us a car, so when the kids came back, we wouldn't have to catch the Metro bus anymore. And I'd get us a house and, most importantly, a good life. And I wrote how much I love everyone in my family, and that I would promise to watch over them and protect them so nothing like this would EVER happen again! So, Mama Dear would be proud of me, and that I would never have to see her cry again . . .*

*With Love,*

*- Manny*

*P.S.*
*I have to keep reminding you that although these are dark days, as long as we have each other, things are never as bad as they seem. And no matter how terrible life may be, or the troubles we may see, even poor people have the right to dream . . .*

*March 2, 1995*

*We visited you in the hospital today at the Harris County Mental Health and Mental Retardation Facility. It was a really long drive across town, and was just as I remembered. The same uneasy energy, patients with vacant stares and staff alternating between glares and suspicion of any and every one, which is fair given their surroundings. In our consult after the visit, a clinician told us that you would act up during your sessions. You spoke of a vast conspiracy, secrets 'they' didn't want to come to the light—you know, same old, same old. But wait, there was one more new twist to the story—you now included me amongst the people who were out to get you. You wouldn't take the medicine, and they wouldn't force it on you. You sleepwalked through the therapy sessions, and they couldn't make you stay for an extended period. You left ill and apparently would be come back ill and pissed. Again. What was I to do?*

*When I first walked in to see you, you were 'bug-eyed', constantly looking around the room, walking from corner to corner, saying that 'they' were watching us. You seemed to be happy I brought the deodorant and hygiene products you asked for. But then you asked me where your babies were, and I had to tell you about Ray and the cops. You immediately yelled, "They gave him my kids?!" I tried to tell you no, we didn't give him anything—he came with the cops and a court paper and took them. But you would not be moved. You got really agitated, and the hospital people came to escort you away. Back to your room I hope and not to some kind of shock treatment, straight jacket, or punishment.*

*As y'all walked away, you asked me, "Why would they do this to me, Mr. Williams? Didn't they know it was my birthday?" I said that, "I'm sorry Mama, I guess they must have forgot . . ." You really stung me with that one, and it sank in how off you really were. Just so you know, your birthday is actually in June, not in March . . .*

*- Manny*

*March 4, 1995*

*In hindsight, I guess I should have seen this a long time ago. When you kept going to the hospital—like every week for stomachaches, food poisoning, migraines, and heart attacks, but they never treated you. They never found anything wrong. They always released you right away, after seeing you in the emergency room. And Ray would take the docs aside and whisper something to them. I always wondered what he had to tell them that was so secret that you could not be in on the conversation. Guess it was something along the lines of, "Sir, my wife truly is sick—just not in that way."*

*And I am really sorry to say this, but you have always been something of a huge drama queen, so I kind of felt like you just wanted the attention. But it has been getting worse and worse, and your claims more and more outrageous in regard to people out to harm you, and us. Aunt Janet said at first, she thought it might have been the kind of depression that some ladies get when they have too many babies back-to-back (very possible since Dominique is four, Dante is three, and Cheyenne just turned two years old). When I came home from school a few, there were holes in the wall, and Aunt Rosalind's hair was all messed up, as if she had been fighting. I decided to ask her about it, and she admitted that you two got into it, and after that she had called the mental health people to commit you this most recent time. That doesn't sound like depression to me, more like aggression . . .*

*Anyways, you got back from the hospital this afternoon. Evidently, they can only keep somebody against their will for involuntary observation for three days. Since you refused to cooperate or take medication, and since they felt you were not a physical threat to harm yourself or others, they let you go. You refused to get a ride from anyone in the family and chose to take the two-hour bus ride home. On cue, after rambling through the house from room to room, you immediately asked where the babies were. I reminded you that Ray had taken them a few days ago, and it was as if this was the first time that you had heard this. Then came the screaming as to how we were working with Ray to conspire against you. My only thought besides the sadness of the situation was how could they have possibly released you like this? What type of treatment are they giving people up there?*

*I told Mama Dear that I wished I was 'normal.' This was one of the few times I was not referring to my face. No, I was actually referring to my outlook* on life. My personality. I wished that I was not a somewhat smart kid, and that I did not 'know better'. That I did not feel moved by yours and other people's pain. How I wished I was no longer motivated to succeed. That I didn't dream in technicolor, and pray in surround sound. That I didn't hide the stuff I want in place of other people needs. That I could stop being a geek and start to run the streets, blow off school, hoop all day, listen to Tupac all night.

She simply looked at me, shook her head, and said, "No you don't, baby, no you don't. This world is full of people like that. And it needs more people like you." Well, there you go.

Mama Dear then tried to remind me that it's important to remember that it was just 'your disease talking.' And, if that's what Mama says, it must be true—because she's always right and never lies to me. I just wish you didn't have to yell and curse so much—and blame us. It's not our fault. It's no one's fault . . . but it's everyone's problem.

I feel these letters are taking somewhat of a different focus now. Not only am I writing to you, but I'm writing for you as well. You're clearly not yourself, Mama—not most of the time at least. That's what gets me. You'll be yelling and screaming for hours on end. And then, all of a sudden, for a few minutes you'll be perfectly fine and peaceful and aware, if that even makes sense. But since you are bad for the majority of the time now . . . I have to wonder which of the two is the 'real' you?

So, I think I kind of need to keep track of this stuff for you for the time being. Maybe as a record of how things were (and are) when you were sick, so you can remember. But, when I tried to talk to you about the promise I made to take care of you, the kids, and Mama Dear, you pretty much brushed me off. But that's ok, I'm not doing it for myself or for the gratitude. But maybe when you feel a little better, I can try to talk to you again about it.

Till that day comes . . .

- Manny

*May 13, 1995*

*So big surprise—Ray filed for divorce. Somebody came and dropped off the papers at the house today. Well, I guess that means it's absolutely over. No chance of y'all getting back together or working this craziness out. I am a little worried at how this might turn out, but everyone insists that you are doing a lot better now (not sure if I completely agree, but maybe a little better) and that judges always give custody to the mother. Consider this as me crossing my fingers on that. But you have to get them back—if there's any justice or God up there.*

*Later on in the evening, I saw you had ripped the divorce papers up and placed them in the trash. Took that about as well as I imagined you would. I noticed that one of the papers said that you were 'psychotic with a history of physical violence.' He's lying about that, right Mama? Because that could definitely hurt your chances of getting joint custody—or any custody for that matter . . . I am so nervous on how this will end up.*

*- Manny*

*May 24, 1995*

*This was a great birthday. Ray let us come over and see the kids for the first time in almost three months. I couldn't believe when he called and offered the invitation. Mama Dear and Janet are saying it's just a ploy to get me on his side and make him not seem like such a bad guy. Well, I couldn't care less. If somebody does a good thing for the wrong reason—at the end of the day, they still did a good thing. And that's all that matters in my book.*

*I asked if I could bring Mama Dear and everyone with me. He said that was fine—but not you. I guess they have some type of restraining order against you after you made some trips up to his house and demanded the kids be returned. Man, that certainly isn't going to help later on in court . . . Janet drove me and Mama out there. Stephanie was left back at home to keep you company, and preoccupied and unsuspicious. The kids looked pretty good. They were happy to see us. We took a ton of pictures, but they have to be developed first before I can show you. Dante had a little flat-top haircut. Dominique is getting super tall. Cheyenne just smiled the whole time. They all wanted to know where Steph and you were. I just told them that you all would be by to see them a different day, so they could get two visits instead of just one—with even more presents (we got them a bunch of stuff at Toys "R" Us). This response seemed to satisfy them, but I can't be completely sure . . .*

*Ray was polite. But it was that weird, guarded kind of polite where you could tell he was really being careful as to what he said. The rest of his family didn't speak to us much at all. But that's okay, because we weren't there for them anyways. Ray said I didn't have to ask for a special occasion to see the kids, just tell him anytime I wanted to stop by. I told him thanks, but I kept my family's warning in the back of my mind that he was trying to get on my good side. I began to ask if you could come out to visit the kids if I promised (as if I could) that you'd act right—but Mama Dear and Janet told me to hush . . .*

*I know the kids couldn't begin to comprehend what's going on right now. Heck, I barely can. But I wish, and I truly do think, that they know how super loved they are. And for them to know that it's always better for too many people to want you than no one at all, right? I wish I could tell them how one day it'll be better when we are all together again. But they are too young to hear all this, and I may even be too young to say it. But I can think it, and I can feel it—because it's all inside me. We hugged and kissed and wished them bye, and then drove on back home.*

*Really wish you could have been here. Next time . . .*

*- Manny*

*June 10, 1995*

*We had our first family reunion today. Wasn't all that festive for many of us. I am really surprised that you decided to come. I mean, seeing as how you don't normally keep in contact much with Mama Dear's relatives (heck, you don't even keep in contact with us that much). And it was really uncomfortable when one of our cousins kept on asking where your other kids were. Janet shooed her away, but the damage was done, and you went off cursing into a corner of the outdoor pavilion—thinking about the one thing we were trying to take your mind off of, if only for one afternoon.*

*Got to see Aunt Erma and her kids. For the longest time, I did not know that she was Mama Dear's sister. I just thought she was somebody's aunt? I didn't even know they were related at first because Mama Dear always called her 'Diggy' on the phone, so I just thought it was one of her old friends from high school or nursing or something. I never put the two together as the same person till I was about eight or nine. She lives really close by, but they just talk on the phone and never hardly meet up face-to-face.*

*I knew that Mama had another sister named Muggins that passed a while back, and a brother named Uncle Pretty Boy, whose real name was Matthew, who had also died a long time ago. They are not talked about much around the house except for the odd mention here and there.*

*All in all, the reunion was okay. I met a ton of people I did not know I was related to. And if I ever saw them again on the street, I doubt that I could recall the fact again . . .*

*But, ya never know.*

*- Manny*

*June 14, 1995*

*The Rockets won their second straight championship tonight! Coach Rudy T., gave the greatest speech ever, and said, "Don't you EVER underestimate the heart of a champion!"*

*That made me think of you Mama. You are going to come back from this, and everyone else will see that they never should have underestimated you.*

*You are my Champion.*

*- Manny*

*July 30, 1995*

*Sorry I haven't written in a while, but I've been working all summer. First through the Houston Works program with the Boys and Girls Club, and then at Drew Middle school as an aide during the summer school session.*

*But more seriously . . . I think I have a girlfriend for the first time in my life.*

*Her name is Shawana—and believe it or not, I actually met her through Uncle June Bug, of all people. He was talking to one girl, and she put her friend on the phone for me to talk to, and she was naturally blown away by my easy, devil may care ways. I'm just happy that I finally found someone that likes me—my scars and all.*

*Your niece (and my older cousin) Naseana once told me that she found you crying to yourself one day, and she asked you why. You replied that you were sad that, "I would never be normal, and find a wife or a job." And people would naturally assume that you were a bad mother and that was the cause of my failures in life.*

*Well, you're really smart, Mama, but I'm sure glad you were wrong on that one. Been now I am working, and have a gal, so that rug has been cut, I suppose. And I'm sure (well, I'm hoping) that you didn't mean it that way . . . but it almost sounded as if you were much more worried that you would be judged harshly as opposed to the fear of your child being lost in the world. Yeah, Naseana must have got that part wrong. Because, sick or not, I must believe that you would not make my life's worries all about you . . . right?*

*With confidence shaken, but not stirred,*

*- Manny*

*November 18, 1995*

*Got my PSAT scores back . . . 1180. Not great, but not terrible. I definitely need to bring it up to 1250 minimum to get that scholarship I want. You know the one—Biomedical Engineering to Texas A&M. I know you've seen the sign in my room, right? The handmade one reading, "I want to go to heaven, but before I get there, I want to go to Texas A&M." My verbal score is golden, but that geometry is what gets me on the math section. It's like they intentionally ask the questions I don't know—those philistines. I'm about to hit the books, posthaste, and let you know the progress I make.*

*See ya around,*

*- Manny*

*December 24, 1995*

*"So, this is Christmas, and what have you done?" That's a line from an unbelievably great John Lennon song that was played for me today at school from this Mexican girl whose name I do not know and had never spoken to before. It's a cool song—but sad as can be for it to be about Christmas. He talks about all the bad things we still have, and that Christmas time, unfortunately, does not make them go away. And I think he has like a black children's choir singing in the background. Mighty cool, Miss Mysterious Mexican Girl. Mighty cool, indeed . . .*

*We (Mama Dear, Janet, Steph, and me) got the kids some Christmas gifts today—including the ones you sent. They liked yours the most—pin-kie swear. Dominique said they had seen you the day before? I'm guessing you caught the bus either to their house or school . . . You gotta be careful with that, Mama. Ray still has that restraining order, and you could get sent to jail! And that would not be in the best interest of your kids at all. But I know you miss them like crazy. It's a tough spot. No need in lying and pretending like it ain't.*

*We're talking to another lawyer right now, so I'll let ya know if we can work a Christmas miracle and get those holiday visitation rights added. And before I forget, I want to add that I am sorry for the way I acted about the jacket you gave me. I just thought it was a bit ugly, and had no idea that you went to the church and registered for gifts for the needy, so you could have something to give your children. The same church that you attended, and had friends that you socialized with and went to school with. I can't imagine how humbling and embarrassing that must have been . . . I am grateful and thankful for anything that you might give me, and all that you do for us. When you get back on your feet, these times will just fade away in the background, and we'll never think of them again.*

*God bless you Mama,*

*- Manny*

*P.S. I liked the way you colored your hair blonde. Don't listen to D.J. and all them. You go girl.*

*February 8, 1996*

*I had my best basketball game ever today. I scored 7 out of my team's 15 points in a three-man game. They could not control me, only pray to contain me—and their prayers were not answered today. I used to just shoot threes and come off picks like my main man Reggie Miller, but I've been watching this boy in college named Allen Iverson and he has these super bad dribbling moves to get to the hole and get floaters—so I added that to my game, too. Man, I miss playing with Ray Ray (Ray's son). Us going out in the rain, or freezing cold, were some of the best times I've ever had in my life. Even with Ray's daughter Tam laughing at us the whole time for being crazy. But it's just not possible right now with the court stuff going on. And depending on how it turns out—it may not be possible ever again . . .*

*Guess what? I found out today that the trust money I got from my lawsuit with the hospital over my burns has been moved because the funds were apparently being mishandled and/or embezzled by the original company. Lovely.*

*And the hits just keep on coming. I'm supposing that's the reason it's only grown from $24,000 to $28,000 when the lawyers said it would be close to $40,000 or $50,000 by my eighteenth birthday. Oh well, just like Mama Dear says, "Don't pay them fools no never mind". I talked to Dominique on the phone today. She is so smart. She dialed all by herself. Don't think I ever did that at five years old, or even had my number memorized. You were gone somewhere on the bus—but Mama Dear and I both told her that you loved her very much and to tell the rest of the kids, too.*

*It can't rain all the time, Mama . . .*

*- Manny*

*June 21, 1996*

*Happy birthday, Mama! My job as a cashier at Krogers is going pretty well, in case you wondering.*

*See ya,*

*- Manny*

*June 23, 1996*

*I guess I just can't stay away . . . I tried to tell myself that I might not be able to write all the time, due to numerous social commitments, charity lunches, and movie premieres, but somehow here I am. First off, there's something you need to know—I wasn't honest with you today. And it's not the first time, as you are well aware.*

*But this time, it was different. It was a good lie. A noble lie. Your birthday gift, that $25 Target Gift Certificate, wasn't really your gift. Well, it partly was, but it mostly wasn't. Follow me? Good. What is your true gift then? Well, you're reading it, lady. And it's not this poorly thought-out letter I'm attempting to write here. It will be a culmination of them. And . . . what will they be? Give me a sec, I haven't exactly finalized my thoughts yet. The idea only came to me while talking to Mama Dear, who you are more prone to refer to as Ms. Vivian Odessa, which is technically her correct name—but a super weird thing to call your mother. I'm just saying. She said that the worst thing about your being sick is that you can't enjoy your children, that you can't see them or the world they are in as it truly is.*

*Now that's what I'm trying to give you—a clearer picture of the world not seen through the false light of your mental illness. And by the time you've read this, I'm praying you'll be able to admit that you were indeed bipolar/manic/schizophrenic—whatever it is the docs have in your hospital records—and not the victim of a conspiracy or collusion or any other diabolical entanglement that starts with the letter 'c.'*

*So that's what I'm offering—a documentation of how things were, are, and will be some day. I'll even bug your nephew (my cousin) Little Greg to fix me up a computer so I can type them down one day.*

*Ambitious— definitely. Worthwhile—to be determined. This undertaking is intended to cover your missing years. Now I realize that you are cognizant (SAT word of the day) of many different things spanning the time frame before this period. Yet, since you became ill, everything has become a jumbled confusion—names, dates, and most importantly—intentions.*

*Mama, I know I've let you down before, but I am going to give this my all. Because it's not just for me, but for you and all of your kids. . . Stephanie, Dante, Dominique, Cheyenne, and myself.*

*We all love you to death and are rooting for you, awaiting the day when you'll be well enough so that a letter won't be required for you to realize this much is true.*

*Once again, Happy Birthday Mama.*

*- Manny*

*June 29, 1996*

*Little Greg came down from Austin and he took me to the movies to see "The Nutty Professor." So dang funny. Eddie Murphy played all the characters from his family. All his stuff is good, and this is way up the list. Only maybe "Coming to America" and "Boomerang" were better—but not by much.*

*Really needed a break from everything, and this hit the spot. Little Greg always shows up at the right time when I need him.*

*- Manny*

*August 2, 1996*

*Good Evening. I always wanted to open up a greeting like that. Now of course it's meant to be said in a Bella Lugosi, Dracula-style voice. Unfortunately, old school horror speech and accents don't play too well in print . . .*

*I wasn't looking to write again tonight, but there has been a minor action I thought I should chronicle: You and I had a blowout today. It was notably one-sided, with you yelling at me. Now don't you fret, I can certainly give just as good as I can take. But that was the old Manny. Now I just walk out during our arguments and retreat to another section of the house. I go in my room, take all the hurtful feelings I'd like to spew, and turn them into a poem, or more recently, a letter such as this. That way I can explore my thoughts, flesh them out, so to speak. It allows the emotions I feel to gain a certain clarity, and therefore seem much more real. Okay, that's enough psychobabble for one night.*

*No hard feelings.*

*- Manny*

*August 29, 1996*

*Okay, here goes. Now, I've been known to overexaggerate once or thrice through the years. But please believe when I say that this Fiona Apple CD I just listened to is the best music I've heard in my life—this side of Tupac, that is. That voice is what puts her amongst the stars. Her picture reveals a thin, pretty little white girl (no offense meant to the thin pretty little white girls of the world) but she sounds so . . . old and battle-weary and . . . real. And I think she's like my age, eighteen or nineteen or so. Her voice is also pretty deep—which is usually not a thing I like in girls not named Demi Moore, but hey, it works for her.*

*In regards to her lyrics, she is a poet in the truest sense. Her songs are both downbeat and touching, melodic and miserable. And one song, track number seven, "Never is a Promise"—I swear they will play this at my funeral. Let me listen to it a few more dozen times before I enshrine her in the Rock Hall of Fame by the time she hits twenty.*

*Usually not so easily amused,*

*- Manny*

*September 1, 1996*

*Interesting thing happened today. In Economics class a few days back, our teacher Mr. Lavergne blew our minds with a 'Theory of Existence' lecture. Jump to present day, and I hear it being discussed on campus in a Philosophy class at the University of Houston. Why am I at UH with my friend Muhammed (aka Air Q due to his basketball skills) skipping class, you ask? Well, we decided we were too smart for high school and would bail to get some higher learning for the day.*

*The theory was originated by a great man whose name escapes me. Now I know you're probably thinking, how great could he have been if I can't even remember his name? Fair enough. He said that pre-birth, we are all blessed with 'Tree of Knowledge' style omniscient power. We know everything inside and out, from Wave Theory to Wonder Woman. Paleontology to Party Planning. But here's the kicker, the inherent trauma of birth—being ripped from our mother's womb—is believed to erase our memories. Complete Tabula Rasa. A form of natal amnesia, if you will. The rest of our lives are then spent trying to remember all that we once had, but ultimately lost . . .*

*Some such as Einstein get closer than others when it comes to science. A person like Van Gogh remembers only a certain segment—art—but he masters it. The rest of us meet varied degrees of success. And it's almost inevitably a fruitless pursuit, because in the eighty or so years we're given, it's impossible to recall a galaxy's worth of information we've lost and then apply it to our existence. Even after we reach the height of our knowledge, in say our fifties or sixties, by then our bodies and minds begin to betray, and ultimately give out on us. This means we are unable to implement what we have learned in our latter years. And as our memory fades, we gradually lose the very knowledge we've spent a lifetime attempting to acquire.*

*Now my spin on it is that pursuit, that effort—or lack thereof—that constitutes the foundation of our lives. Our characters and personalities are dependent on what parts we remember, and in how much detail. Drug addicts and criminals would be those who realize early on that they would never get it all back, say what the hell, and do their own thing instead. At the other end would be your Mother Theresa and Princess Diana-like figures who recognize the same thing, but they try to even the playing field for others who came into the world with more disadvantages than themselves. Nearly everyone I've ever told this to laughs at me, and you may as well . . . but I happen to feel that it perfectly describes my existence. It encompasses what I'm all about. Trying to remember everything in this mad world I possibly once might have known. And that miraculous chase, that never-ending race, is what I live for.*

*If by chance you ever find out this philosopher's name somewhere, could you let me know? I'm quite certain that I used to know it, but it would appear that it has somehow slipped my mind . . .*

*Talk to you later. 'I've got dreams to remember.'*

*- Manny*

*September 7, 1996*

*Oh God No. Tupac was shot today. Everybody thought it was a joke at first . . . But then when we all found out it was real . . . Had to be some type of set-up or something. The guys were waiting for him when he was driving away from the Tyson fight in Vegas. It's just stupid, man. These are supposed to be musicians, and they are out here acting like wannabe gangsters. He went to a performing arts high school with the girl from A Different World for God's sake.*

*I just hope he's okay. He made it through the last shooting, but there's only so many times you can beg for a miracle.*

*Super sad,*

*- Manny*

*September 13, 1996*

*Pac Died Today. On 97.9, they played his music all night. Started off with "Dear Mama," which is a classic and got him a lot of fans and respect with the older crowd, but they should have come with that "Life Goes On" first. In it, he talks about his own funeral and how he wants it to go down. There would not have been a dry eye in the city.*

*I wrote him a letter while he was in jail but never had the nerve to send it. Figured it never would have gotten read, and he wouldn't have cared anyway. But turns out, he read all those letters. He said in an interview that some even had money for him from little kids.*

*The basics of my letter: Calm the hell down! I said that he was too talented and meant too much to all people of color around the world to be acting that way. That kids needed him. That I needed him. That our community could not stand to have another great voice—only to lose it entirely too early. That nobody was certain—not even him— what kind of greatness he was capable of, but that would surely be something fun to discover over the years. Yeah, he probably wouldn't have cared anyway . . .*

*- Manny*

*October 20, 1996*

*My Geometry teacher Mrs. May loves her some Lakers. She usually never talks to us about non-school stuff, but heard us talk about basketball and jumped in the conversation to everyone's surprise. She swears up and down that their new rookie he came straight out of high school is going to be the best player ever? I have no idea what she is basing that on. He just turned 18, is skinny, and was hurt already during the Summer League games. He'll be lucky to get off the bench this year because their team is good, and he will play behind Eddie Jones who is a good shooting guard. I don't see it.*

*Ms. May was actually Little Greg's teacher as well when he went here, and he said she was a great teacher – but super mean. He was not wrong. But she is strict and don't take any nonsense, so it's not exactly mean, as it is her job. Strictly Business with this lady. And she just happens to teach the one class I am clueless in . . .*

*November 8, 1996*

*Got my SAT Scores Back—1320! What do you know about that?! I'm talking about National Achievement, full ride to college, having a great life. 660 down the line between Math (91 percentile) and Verbal (92 percentile). Consistent as can be. If I transfer downstairs from the magnet Engineering program at Booker T., I can graduate in January. Probably could graduate now—I have more than enough credits.*

*My future's so bright, I gotta wear shades.*

*- Manny*

*November 19, 1996*

*Thanksgiving is just around the corner. I have decided to turn down all the outside (Houston, that is) scholarships I have received. Mama Dear has been riding me, but nonetheless, I know it's the right thing to do.*

*There were Lehigh and Drexel reps (cute one named Toni) for the N.A.C.M.E. engineering programs in Pennsylvania asking me to sign up today. A Dartmouth rep had asked about me specifically as well, Mr. Bruce, our counselor, said. Maybe if I knew that I wouldn't have skipped it. Nah, too cold up there. And then there is my formerly beloved Texas A&M. They yanked my full ride for no rhyme or reason. And then comes the kicker—they had the nerve to tell me to please still consider their school because of how great it is and how highly ranked in the national publications. Umm yeah, I knew all that boss—it's why I wanted to go there to begin with and needed that damn scholarship.*

*But it has to be due to the 'Hopwood Case', where they only let in minorities with low scores—figuring the others can get money elsewhere. Because my numbers, extra curriculars, and essays are better than any of the kids at school who got to keep their scholarships. I know of at least three who got full rides.*

*On a different note, I just heard the new Nas album and it blew my mind! He uses imagery and metaphors like he is teaching an advancement placement class on poetry. I could listen to this all day, every day. No replacing Pac, but he Nas in his own lane, and doing his own thing. My holy trinity for rappers is Pac, Nas, and Scarface. I think Scarface is in fact (besides being a local boy), the only rapper everyone can agree they like with no hating going on. He's got that great deep voice and dramatic delivery. Awesome lyrics too. Plus, he ain't East or West coast, so he gets love from both sides.*

*- Manny*

*December 1, 1996*

*Thanksgiving was horrible. Just thought you should know. Anyhow, a question that often keeps me up at night happened to . . . kept me up tonight. The existential quandary, If I wasn't here, where would I be? You know, the "what if I were born in a different place or point in time" dilemma. I don't mean a vastly different point in history—such as ten or twenty years forward or backwards on the timeline. Oh no, I'm talking about one day, maybe even one hour. Do you think that could have changed things? Because I do.*

*Take this scenario for instance. What if you had been home instead of at school when I turned up ill after I accidentally ingested poisoned at my day care? Or was intentionally poisoned depending on your level of faith in humanity is, because how can a six-month-old baby find his way into poison unattended? There's almost no chance I would have went to a teaching hospital for my recovery, as opposed to a more established institution. There would not have been any third-year medical students working on me; no inexperienced nurse to run an IV in my head when the arm would not take. And therefore, no second and third degree burns on 75 percent of my scalp and face when something went wrong with the IV. No*

*screams for weeks on end as my head turned charcoal black and then bal-*
*looned to twice its normal size. These are some of the things that cross my*
*mind Mama—every single time I look into a mirror.*

*But you never know—it could have been worse. Rosalind told me an*
*older couple had a sick child in the same intensive care pediatric ward at*
*Hermann Hospital as me. They were in their late forties or early fifties,*
*and felt blessed to have a child in their life. He had a condition which*
*caused an enlargement and deformity to his head. But all Rosalind could*
*remember were his eyes. The biggest, brownest, puppy dog eyes one could*
*ever hope to see. That little boy didn't have the chance to grow up in pov-*
*erty, be picked on at school, curse his parents for the gift of life, or lay it all*
*out in his late teens in an open-heart diary to his sick mother. You may not*
*remember, but a nurse dropped that little boy on his head one day while*
*feeding him, and he died within an hour, so she tells me.*

*Since hearing that story from, I now have two things that keep me up*
*in the late-night hours.*

*Still sad . . . yet grateful,*

*- Manny*

*December 26, 1996*

*Mama Dear and I had our first fight ever today. It concerned me refus-*
*ing to speak to June Bug at Christmas. He got high, jumped on, and*
*tried to beat up Jamon, and when I broke it up, he tried to fight me, too.*
*Jamon eventually broke his dad's arm, and the fallout was immense. Our*
*argument began the same old way—with Mama Dear saying that I was*
*wrong for being 'that way' and I shouldn't hold it against June Bug. Um,*
*you mean I shouldn't hold it against him that he took several swings at*

*me? I promptly informed her that she had no right to judge me. And then I went completely off because she made a direct hit on a raw nerve. For sixteen years, I have wanted to be treated like her son, instead of just her grandson, and I felt she should have wanted this too. This is undoubtedly why Uncle June Bug always managed to piss me off with his drinking and outbursts.*

*They say that drugs and alcohol only bring out the worst parts of your personality that were always there, and I wholeheartedly believe that. These traits are merely content to do their thing in the background of your id/ego/subconscious until you supersize their power with the mood enhancer of your choice.*

*For the life of me, I could not figure out why Mama Dear would not put him out on his ass. He talked to her (and me) like dirt. He lied, stole, and used/sold drugs at her home, and so forth. Her reply to me was that she could no sooner put him out than she could put you out Mama. I told her there was no way those two situations were remotely similar. Where he chose to get messed up every night at the same bat time, your condition was genetic (at least partially). Mama Dear refused to acknowledge this.*

*I told her that she always gripes about me not staying over at her house as much—well he was the reason why. I needed to make a decision quickly about housing for my freshman year at college. I never intended to stay on campus, but now told her that in no uncertain terms that if she had made June Bug leave, I would have stay with her (and you and the kids by extension) like she wanted me to, and not moved out. But she did not bite at my offer. I called on her to remember her old saying of, "The path you refuse is the path you should choose." I told her not to push me away—the one who loved her—while embracing someone who continually hurts her. I screamed that she did not know what she was doing, that I was the good one—the one who didn't drink or smoke, mistreat women, or hit children. How could she ever choose him over me? Well, as it turns* out, quite easily. Monster or not, he was still her son. And just as June Bug loved to prophetically tell me in his drunken stupors, "You could grow up to be rich, successful, and smart, but there is one thing you could never be—Vivian's real son." But again, my pleas came to no avail. I guess all girls really do have a thing for bad boys . . .

When I stormed out that day, she was in tears. And if I had to quantify it, I'm sure I had just hurt her as much in that instance as he ever did. Yeah, me. The good one. And since I'm in a confessional type mood, there is an even greater reason why I stopped staying with her, besides my louse of an uncle. That reason being that it was much too painful to see her.

Through time and observation, I've realized that I am, indeed, not her son. And that our relationship is not the same—what she and I have, that is. She has devoted space in her heart for her two fallen angels, June Bug and You. She begs and she borrows for y'all. She feeds your children, covers your mistakes, and excuses your failures without fail.

I'm just a foot soldier in pursuit of that mission, and coming face to face with that is unbearable.

- Manny

February 26, 1997

Ray is Dead. It's like three o'clock in the morning. DJ woke me up to tell me. With him, I figured it was just another one of his morbid jokes. But he swore it wasn't. I am sad he passed, but I would be lying if I were to say that I was not ecstatic that the kids would be coming home and we all would be reunited.

Our family has told me a lot of negative things they say Ray said about you in court, and you told them in secrecy that he did to you . . .

but I don't know . . . To me, I never saw him as Public Enemy #1. But every one of us has different sides they show to different people, so anything is possible.

It seems Ray was driving with a friend down the highway when they ran into the back of an eighteen-wheeler in the early morning hours. He was dead on contact. His friend had the top of his head sliced off, hung on for a little while, and then passed away. I've heard it was an accident— that the truck was stopped on the road with no hazard lights on and they ran into it by mistake. I've also heard they were drunk and or high, were speeding, and just couldn't stop in time to avoid the accident. Yet, regardless of how it came to pass, the death of a man disliked by many still has meaning to those who did care for him. And that begins with the five children he left behind (I'm including Tam and Ray Ray, not me and Steph).

One of my favorite movies of all time is The Usual Suspects. In it, Kevin Spacey says "The greatest trick the devil ever pulled, was convincing the world he didn't exist."

Why do I think of Ray in connection with this movie? Well, because I liked him. I liked him quite a bit. And much like Detective Kujan with Verbal Kint, I chose to believe everything he told me, unquestioningly. Why shouldn't I? He gave me rides to school, bought me video games, and took me and Steph out to dinner and the movies twice a month on his payday. And material things aside, it was because he stuck around. I'd seen many of your 'male suitors' come and go—and the go was usually when they got a hint that you had two small children. You had not worked full time in years, was living at your mother's house, but he spent time with us and didn't make us feel guilty about it—hell yeah, I liked him. And that made it hurt all the much worse. Like when Kujan discovered someone he trusted, someone he knew was 'dumber' than him, had played him all along.

You met in the late 1980s at Lloyd's, a hole-in-the-wall club close to Mama Dear's house. The kind of local establishment that is deemed *necessary so money can stay in the community, yet inevitably turns into a liquor/drug dungeon with quickness. This leads to nonstop police patrolling, then raids, then the eventual closing of said establishment. Thus, leading locals to protest how there is no place to go within their own community and calling for another like club to be built. And the same place will be rebuilt, but with a little white sign in the corner window stating that it is currently 'Under New Management'.*

*Ray was a city sanitation worker, just like your father James L. Janet said that your dad actually knew of Ray from the job, and he did not particularly care for him. Game Recognizes Game, I suppose. Ray was divorced with two kids of his own, Ray Ray who was four years younger than me, and Tam who was two years older than me. When he started bringing them around, I was overjoyed. Actual friends. People of my own age who were not related to me yet chose not to judge or laugh at me. Furthermore, I'd always wanted a little brother, and Ray Ray fit the bill (especially since I never got to see my cousin Jamon). He loved basketball, videogames, and girls. Good stuff. I actually got my love of the game from him. He was small for his age—but he was cold-blooded on the court. Watching him school grown men, time after time, inspired me to get out there and try. We played on weekends, holidays, after funerals—you name it. Ray had visitation rights on every other weekend, and me and his boy were inseparable. He was always Jordan, while I was Reggie Miller or Hakeem (whose destruction of David Robinson in the '95 Finals is the greatest thing I have ever witnessed). Tam kept to herself mostly. She kind of thought of me as a geek, which was fair play, seeing as how I was a geek. Yet she always spoke—if spoken to—and really seemed to like you. Y'all would go shopping, or you'd help her with her hair and makeup.*

*So here I was soon enough, twelve years old, with a stepdad, two new siblings, you happy, and everything great in the state of Denmark. Of* course, it could never last. But at that point in time, these things were as good as good was going to get. Stephanie loved Ray, called him Daddy and everything. You know, she never really knew hers, even though Arthur Lee literally stayed right next door to Mama Dear. But then again, bad blood doesn't begin to describe what went on between our two families—more like infected blood. I mean, you did shoot and paralyze him after all; not the kind of thing that rolls off one's back, to say the least.

But he was a drug addict and a woman beater, and instant karma—by way of a 38 special—caught up with him. However, his family still feels that you were in the wrong. When you went to the hospital to visit him after the guilt set in, his brother hit you in the mouth and damn near broke your jaw. I still remember that . . .

Arthur Lee was rather short—5'5" on a good day—but he was unbelievably strong. One of those bodies chiseled in juvenile only to have the finishing touches carved out by the penitentiary. But then again, there is no hot yoga in the hood, I guess. He was in and out since he was twelve for stealing cars, fighting cops, etc. He was one of those guys where no matter how outlandish the story you heard about him, you could pretty much imagine it was probably true. He had an uncle named Popeye who was short, stocky, and always squinted, just like the spinach-loving cartoon dude. Popeye always spoke to me every day after school—for some reason he called me 'Benji,' and I don't know why, but it stuck. He'd give me a quarter on most days as well; but after I grew up, he'd be the one asking me for money—but now it was a dollar. Inflation, I suppose . . .

But he was also a drunk. I'm talking every-single-day. Completely Lit. Mama Dear said the only time he opened his mouth to speak was if he was 'loaded'. But Unlike June Bug, he appeared to be a happy drunk. I've never seen him yell or curse in all my years—but I've never lived with him either. And I've heard that some pretty horrible things went down in that house next to ours. But I choose to believe he was not a part of that scene.

*And if that puts a spotlight on my naiveté or sense of adult reasoning, then so be it. As I've said before, I'll forever be a dreamer.*

*So that little excursion brings us to the last reason why I liked Ray—he was not Arthur Lee. Or my nonexistent father, as far as that goes. He stayed. He had three kids with you, and he still stayed. For a while, that is.*

*But now let's go to the other side of the man I used to like, but learned to be indifferent toward. For one, he tricked me. I mean in films, I love diabolical villains who have depth and layers to their character. But in real life I prefer my bad guys to in the purest form. I'm talking black clothes wearing, mustache-twirling glee. Not someone who pretends to be a new urban 'Stepfather of the Year' and lures you into a false ideal. One of my favorite Shakespeare quotes says, "One may smile, and smile, and be a villain." Only now do I truly understand what he was talking about.*

*Here goes. You and Ray had spats like all couples do, but they were pretty explosive. He liked to go out and partake in certain activities—drink, gamble, do drugs—the usual. Later info would indicate that he also had several women on the side while you were married, but I only know of one for sure—Becky. Ray told me flat out when I was thirteen that he, "once had a drug and drinking problem," before finding God. However, it soon became extremely clear now that those were habits he just couldn't shake. And if he had painstakingly found God, he rather carelessly lost him again . . . Remember when we used to drop him off on Saturday mornings at a building where he would catch a bus with other dudes to go work? Well, at the time I thought it was like volunteer work or overtime. But during your divorce trial I found out it was supervised work detail as part of his probation.*

*He was a garbage collector with the city for at least fifteen years, making good money. But every now and then, large sums would come up missing. Then, one night he came home without his paycheck, it all came to a head. He ducked in around midnight, then, minutes later, stormed out of the new house y'all had just rented near Eisenhower High School.*

We got a call around 4am that he was in jail. You then started making the rounds on the phone to try and raise his $5000 bail. It seems that he was out shooting dice and drinking, and was messing with a girl that rolled him for his paycheck. He then came home to hunt down his friend on the phone and left to go borrow his sawed-off shotgun. He caught up with the girl's 'boyfriend' (and by boyfriend, I mean pimp) and demanded his money back. The businessman refused, Ray shot, the gun backfired, and the law came shortly thereafter. This event basically served as a watershed point in the unraveling of your marriage. Due to that lost check, subsequent probation costs, and lawyer fees, we were evicted from the nice house that we had only been in for six months.

One of the true-blue signs of poverty is constantly moving. I can recall us living at no less than eleven different addresses by the time I was twelve. There were row houses and apartments, duplexes and single-family homes, rented rooms and charitable accommodations. They were on Yale and Bunzell, Antoine and Little York, Arncliffe and Lockwood, West Gulf Bank and Antoine again, and always, always there was good old Dollywright, with Mama Dear.

The house we lost with Ray was by far the nicest we had ever lived: paved driveway, vaulted ceilings, an intercom system that was wired for every room, and a separate bedroom for everyone in the house. That alone was the stuff of ghetto dreams. Far away from the small house that Mama Dear offered with shared beds, roaches, and addicts lurking around every other street corner. But alas, it was not meant to be. And, anyway, there were some sad, scary things that went down in that beautiful house. It was the site of your worst breakdowns. And you've had some whoppers over the years, so trust me when I say it was bad. I'm talking you holding us out of school for two weeks at a time because you thought someone was following the bus. Then there was you throwing away $200 in groceries because you were certain they were 'contaminated.' There was the constant checking of the telephone for 'taps,' looking up the chimney for Ray's mistress, walking around with a loaded Browning 9mm at all times of the day and night. I'm not even going to talk about the 22-caliber pistol you kept in the fanny pack around your waist, or Ray's AK-47 that you hid under the bed.

Your lowest moment—the one where I first realized you were not merely quirky or eccentric—occurred in the nights following Ray's arrest. You'd wake us up all throughout the night, end eventually had us come and sleep with you in the closet. It seems that was the only place where the omnipresent 'they' could not read your thoughts. Since I was twelve, you even allowed me to stand guard outside the door every so often—but only with the handguns. I was told the AK would have to wait until my next birthday. Always safety first with you Mama.

Now I initially kept quiet about your weird behavior. I suppose most kids do the same when faced with an unusual predicament in the home front—be it abuse, homelessness, or mental instability. The old "don't speak of it, and perhaps it will go away," theory. But eventually, I could not help myself. I told Mama Dear, and this was the first step in everyone in our family finding out. Poor Granny, she couldn't keep a secret if my life depended on it. At first you kept your game face on, refusing to show your true self. But in time, your illness eventually came to light. You would ask your sisters if they noticed any unusual cars while on the road; you'd hold multiple conversations with yourself in front of people. And there was one Christmas dinner where you demanded to see photo identification from everyone in the room to prove they were not impostors spying on you.

You then accused Mama Dear of not being the 'Real' Vivian, saying your mother died in a car crash as a teenager. It was shocking and sad for everyone to witness. There were bits of truth interspersed with your paranoid delusions. There you were, the self-proclaimed 'sharpest' member of our family (until Little Greg came along). High school salutatorian, a master's candidate within a few classes of finishing, etc. And now you were a daughter who no longer recognized her mother. This was our collective *breaking point. Janet paid for you to go see a shrink, Rosalind took the two smallest kids to her house, and the rest of us stayed with Mama.*

*You were gone about a week and a half, and it seemed as if all signs were good in regard to you getting healthier. They had you on two separate medications that appeared to level out your mood swings. And most importantly, you were able to rest. The rest that a lady who has three kids in less than four years so desperately needs. The docs gave you every label in the book—and why wouldn't they? Your delusions were definite signs of paranoid schizophrenia. And the mood swings pointed to manic depression. Then there's the aforementioned postpartum depression that was suspected all along. If there was a mental diagnosis that somewhat fit your symptoms, they gave it to you. Being cut off from your family (although self-induced), from the shame of how you were living only exasperated your problems.*

*Now many of us speculated that your personality began to change after Arthur Lee's shooting. You were withdrawn, remorseful, and to top it off, you'd been let go from your good city job as a speech pathologist. And for a true woman about town such as yourself, this was the final straw, so to speak. You loved to be the big shot—flaunting your job, cash flow, degree. You'd take your friends out on expensive dinners downtown, only to drive right back to the ghetto where you lived. With the same people you would later talk down to. Irony, karma, tragedy, whatever, you get the gist.*

*In the back of my mind, I always wondered if any of your siblings, in some small way, or in some small part—while not happy about your predicament—were at least a bit, shall I say 'vindicated' in your down fall. As if to say, "I always knew she wasn't that smart. Or better than me. She was just luckier than me." And in helping you out, they were proving themselves to be, in fact, the 'greater person.' Maybe not. Maybe so.*

*Now back to my tale. Well, we lost that house on Arncliffe after Ray went to jail. Then you began therapy, and I felt as if the storm circling all of our heads might actually pass. After you calmed down a bit, you started opening* up to Janet and Rosalind—and the things you told them, they are still hard for me to accept, as they were recently relayed to me for the first time.

You said Ray was the one instigating all of your paranoia. That he told you about government spies and your own family plotting on you. Now Mama Dear and your sisters took this as gospel from day one. I mean, they never felt Ray was good enough for you—that you had married a man lacking the intellect and culture for a woman such as yourself. Sounds kind of like the things that I heard Mama Dear's family told her about your daddy. However, I couldn't believe it. I wouldn't believe it. No way—you were the crazy one. You were the one that ruined your life, broke our new family apart, and made herself the center of attention once again. In my mind, Ray couldn't be the bad man. I mean, I had seen more than my fair share of bad men in my life, and I could not accept one more. Especially one that I happened to like . . .

I think it was Christmas of 1991, the first that Ray spent at Mama Dear's, in which he gave you a rather dubious gift—a Beretta 9mm semi-automatic handgun. It was brand new, black on chrome, and probably cost about $400 dollars. Ray could not understand when everyone in the house began to crack up. First D.J., then June Bug, and Mama Dear even got a chuckle or two in I believe. Ray then nervously laughed himself, not knowing what everyone found so funny—the inside joke he was yet to be privy to. D.J. put it bluntly, "You do know what happened the last time Selita had a gun, right?" He said he did not. I was kind enough to finally clue him in—that you shot your last boyfriend. Talk about a Christmas icebreaker.

But as it would turn out, although you despised him, wished—and many times threatened—death upon Ray (and many others), a bullet to the abdomen would be the last thing he would have to worry about.

Cheyenne's fourth birthday was three days ago. At least he got to see that. Please Lord let this story have a happy ending . . .

*- Manny*

*February 27, 1997*

*Hold off on that happy ending. We went to Ray's father's house and they would not let us take the kids! I know you don't believe us (based on your yelling and screaming and cursing), but I swear to God that is what happened.*

*They have No Right. The father is deceased and you're the mother— end of story. Now Ray's older brother Calvin said he's their godfather and he will continue the custody dispute on Ray's behalf. This is some straight up lunacy. I'm really sorry things didn't work out like I told you they would, Mama.*

*I'm really sorry.*

*- Manny*

*March 5, 1997*

*True to his wayward word, Calvin has filed for custody. So now we have a whole new fight on our hands . . . And more money that Janet, Mama Dear, and Rosalind have to pay to fight this. I'm working more hours at Kroger so I can pitch in too—though it won't be much. It's going to take a whole lot, they say. I need you to have faith—even if I ain't exactly running over with it myself right now.*

*We decided to use a play from their book by having Mama Dear apply for temporary guardianship. Since you are so unpredictable, and they were basing their case on this fact, we would run an end around basically not objecting to this point. And with Mama as guardian, the kids would be right there with you. Through the first round of depositions, you were not needed, but as time went by, it became apparent that if you did not eventually show up, then the judge would find for Ray's family in absentia.*

*So today I begged, and I pleaded. And I cried, and I threatened. And I nearly tore your door down. Your reply to me was to, 'Mind my own business,' and that these children were "None of my concern." I could not believe you had the nerve to speak to me like that. Your children were not my concern. We're talking about my brothers and sisters here. Who I had been helping to take care of since I was thirteen—using my job money to buy groceries, and diapers and . . . Me, who had been falling over himself to thank Janet and Rosalind for paying for your doctors and lawyers while you were cursing them out and fighting them every step of the way. But that was my downfall. Me working with your sisters and lawyer equated to me automatically working against you. I was no longer your son, but just another enemy in your eyes. D.J. had to pull me back. I broke away, and he had to come and get me again. In no way do I think I would have hit you, but I'm damn near certain I would have shaken you till I cleared some cobwebs out of your cloudy mind. But the end result is that we won custody back—so most is forgiven, but never forgotten.*

*- Manny*

*March 9, 1997*

*The Notorious B.I.G. was killed today. I definitely chose my side between him and Pac, but this is Stupid, and Senseless, and has To Stop. Nobody should be dying over songs, or where they live, and how has the "best crew". Let alone young, talented black men who have families that love them, and millions of fans, especially kids that look up to them.*

*- Manny*

March 13, 1997

*I sing because I'm happy . . . And more importantly, I sing because we got to visit the kids at Calvin's today! It's an extremely nice place, but it's way out in Channel View. I guess they picked the brother with the most money and the farthest distance from a bus line to go for custody to keep you at bay.*

*The kids seemed pretty good. The girls had nice dresses on and slacks for Dante.*

*There are other kids of Calvin's in the house, so they have someone to play with. But still. it's not where they belong. Calvin knows. And he knows that we know he knows it. I actually just got off from work. It's like 11:45 at night—Kroger is working me to the bone. Whatever happened to child labor laws and all that jazz? What's worse, by the time I pay bus fare, eat a small deli lunch, and give my friend Chris from school the odd $5 here and there for gas, and you money for the bus and whatever else you need—there is absolutely, positively no loot left in the old wallet. I think I end up owing my job like $50 a week?! I've been falling asleep in Physics and Calculus . . . and come to think of it . . . I'm pretty tired . . . right . . . now . . .*

*Fighting Mr. Sandman until the day I die,*

*- Manny*

April 16, 1997

*They tried, and they tried, but they could not keep a good woman down! You won custody, Mama! The kids will be home in a day's time. They had a witch of a lawyer. She tried to trip me up on the stand, but yours truly held his own.*

*It was weird to see Tam and Ray Ray on the other side of the fence. But again, our new lawyer Tracy (who is actually related to Maxine, Mama Dear's niece) said that they did not say anything bad about you in their testimony. And I think Tam actually said that her family was wrong and that the kids should be with you.*

*Good for her. They will be home within a day according to the judge. Now where to put them? Mama Dear's house ain't getting no bigger at this stage of the game. So, I guess we'll have to sleep double and triple to a bed again. A small price to pay indeed.*

*Truly a day the Lord has made!*

*- Manny*

*May 5, 1997*

*Biggest week in my life to date by far. Shawana and I actually broke up over going to the prom. I wanted to go with her, but I still don't hardly know how to drive, let alone make it out to Galena Park by myself at night. Not enough money to chip in for a limo with her friends. I guess I/ she/whoever ended it because I was just . . . I don't know . . .*

*My high school graduation was tonight at Texas Southern, your old college. I told everyone I would get lost coming off the stage, and I'll be a fool if I didn't. They tell you to walk off, but they don't tell you where to walk off to. I saw Jeheil, my old friend from St. Rose of Lima. That was the Catholic elementary school you got me into, until the money ran out after you lost your job. It was pretty interesting—private vs. public school. Some differences, such as much more prayers, of course. Some things remained the same, like getting beat up and made fun of . . . Some nuns like Sister Kaderka were unbelievably nice. Others, not so much. One (Sister M.) told me I was ignorant and possessed horrible grammar and English skills. Fun times. Some were carefree, others a little too carefree—nuns in rehab for alcoholism, priest drove a car through school grounds. All "allegedly" of course.*

*I never really knew how poor we were until a few of the kids there pointed it out. How old our car was compared to everyone else's. How I wore the same clothes often, with few variations, week after week. How I always brought lunch instead of buying it like the others. Dang, those jokers were pretty perceptive. If they worked on their prayer's half as much as their bullying, one of them might have made Cardinal one day.*

*Jeheil had on a navy suit, or was it an ROTC outfit? I know he played football and basketball at Eisenhower and was really good, but had no idea that he was going to enlist. We lost touch completely after fourth or fifth grade. He used to pick me for sports, even though I was terrible, and stood up for me when others made fun of me. He, Marcus, and I were three of the only black kids in the entire school. But even heroes deserve a break, and eventually, he took a permanent one from me, which I don't hold against him whatsoever.*

*He kind of waved, but he didn't speak. Just like the "Epic of Gilgamesh" says, "It's impossible to keep the names of those friends we have lost." That's a paraphrase, by the way.*

*One of our cousins, Peter (along with his sister Kara), went to St. Rose also, and then later to Eisenhower, where he too was a football star. He didn't speak to me, but maybe once or twice all my years there. Peter went to school up north I think and eventually became a teacher (radicalized and married to a white girl per family gossip). I think Kara played basketball and became a model or something. Peter stopped by Mama Dear's house one day a week a so ago to speak to her, and he asked about me. This was at least eight or more years since we last spoke. The 'good side' of the family doesn't often reach out to the 'poor relations,' ya know . . . But I was not there to see him and only heard of the visit later. Had no idea he even remembered me after all these years . . .*

*On even more of a down note (yeah, I'm just Mr. Sunshine today, huh?), you are still not changing too much in personality now that the kids are back. I really thought you would 'snap out of it' and go back to your old self. But you still curse and fight, see and hear things no one else does, and all the other strange stuff. I'm really thinking that you are going to need some long term serious professional help before everything is said and done.*

*Hoping for the best—yet always prepared for the worst.*

*- Manny*

*May 18, 1997*

*It's late, and I'm beat. Not the greatest way to open an entry, but hey, what are ya gonna do? Dante came from school with a fundraiser packet and a school picture form. They really know how to clock those dollars in grade school. I never was really into taking pictures myself. Many disfigured people aren't. But I have taken my share over the years, and like all parental types, I'm known to play favorites.*

*Without a doubt, my favorite would have to be the picture where I'm six weeks old. Rosalind said I looked so light-skinned back then that when she tried to walk me around the hospital floor, she was approached and asked where she got that 'white' baby from? Pure comedy. Oh yeah, my hair was wavy, my waist was small, and if you pay attention, you'll notice there's not a scar to be found on me at all.*

*I love to show this to people after I've gotten to know them for a good long while—the ones who don't gawk at me incessantly or pepper me with questions over my appearance. After I reached nine or ten, I could start to see it a mile away. Some ask straightaway; others get someone else to bring it up in their place. Some hope if they linger around long enough, that I'll unburden* my soul and confess all, Jimmy Swaggart-style. And others merely blurt it out, a betrayal of their home training, a cold shoulder to their better judgment. Yet whatever their approach, they all want to know, and I really don't blame them for it anymore. It's human nature, our need to know all. To get an explanation for the unexplained. They need something as a point of reference—an admonition, cautionary tale for family and friends, if you will.

I heard when I was first in the hospital, nurses would come by and tell you, "Oh what a beautiful baby you have." And then after I was burned, they would come by and say, "Oh what a blessed baby you have." The difference is not lost on me . . .

"What happened to you? Who did that? How long ago? That's a burn, no doubt. Nah, he must have been jumped. I heard his dad did it to him. Gulf War, right?" Trust me, I've heard them all. Many times, I'll give a response, but it's just as likely I won't. Much like a great golf shot, it all begins with the approach. You've seen me watching golf on TV all of a sudden, right? Well, it's because Tiger Woods is The Truth. Nuff said. And no matter how they ask, the subtext will continue to be the same: "Not to be rude young man/son/bro, but if it's not too much trouble, could ya possibly tell me how I could avoid something similar happening to myself/my child/my dog?"

And I'm only human, so of course it still gets to me every now and then. Those are the days I flip open my photo album and glance upon my favorite picture. And to those who make it into my inner circle, I'll let them take a look at it as well—especially the girls I go out with and such. This picture is something of a saving grace for me. It means something. It proves something. What? That I wasn't always different. That I was not born an outcast. That if she saw fit to love me, and we had kids, they would not share my damaged looks. That our children could probably be ok looking, possibly be great looking, but never, ever, grow up to be less than. More than likely.

Lightning will never strike me twice.

- Manny

May 24, 1997

Another birthday for little old me. Little Greg came down and gave me a Macintosh computer for my birthday to use for college. So that's why this letter is typed as opposed to hand written. He's still having a beast of a time with those fools up in Austin. The racism is strong up there, especially in the computer field that he works in at Motorola. I told him that he should come down here, we could go to UH together, he could finish his degree, and tell them all to go you know where. But he ain't having none of it. Guess he ran out from H-town when he was eighteen, and only likes to make guest appearances from now on. It sure would be fun, though, if he changed his mind.

DJ rented *What's Eating Gilbert Grape* for me, a movie I love. Maybe because it's a pretty woeful tale of a young dude taking care of a family he'd rather not. Maybe because D.J. always says he thought Johnny Depp's character reminded him a lot of me. I used to brush it off, but now, I see it as pretty much fact.

DiCaprio was pretty dang good too—got an Oscar nomination even—but this is still Depp's story as far as I am concerned. It's how Johnny/Gilbert cared for his misfit family the best way he knows how, while being stuck in a town he longs to get away from. He keeps doing the 'right thing' by not bailing out on his people, but it gets harder and harder as time goes on to play the part of the good guy. Man, can I ever relate.

Sticking around gives me a ready-made excuse if I never amounted to much in life. I can blame it on you, say it was the kids, the stress of it all. Like Doc said in *Tombstone* about Johnny Ringo, "Poor soul. He was just too high strung. The stress of this world was just more than he could bear." Well, no more. I refuse to allow myself to fall into that pity vortex. I *am* gonna do it. I *will* make something out of myself. And when I do, it's going to be all the more impressive because I did stick around as opposed to moving away and high-tailing it out, though I want to a hundred times over. And I'm not going to lose who I am to get there—wherever 'there' may be. I will keep on being a good son, a great brother, a provider, a protector, and a grandson that his grandmother can brag about for all her livelong days.

Gilbert has a great line in the movie where he says, "There's a difference between staying because you have to and staying because you want to." That could definitely be a defining quote for my life. It's taken me a few years and several screenings, but I finally understand what that difference is. I was wondering if maybe you forgot to say Happy Birthday to me today? But no worries, I know you were thinking it all along.

Talk to you later,

- Manny

∽◌⌣

July 5, 1997

Stephanie's dad, Arthur Lee, died today. Mama Dear told me when I got home from work. He was pretty young, like thirty-five or so. It was pneumonia, I think. I heard that people in wheelchairs get it a lot. I don't think Mama Dear is letting Steph go to the funeral next week. Still too much bad blood after you shot him ten years ago. Not sure how Steph is taking it. She hardly knew him, and only spoke to him a hand full of times that I know of, even though he literally lives on the other side of the fence of our house . . .

- Manny

August 30, 1997

I started at the University of Houston last week—and school is kicking my behind. I was the last one to get to our dorm room, so I got the noisiest bed, closest to the door. My suitemates are both white—Sean, a skinny Chicago dude who is very well-spoken and an English major, I think. Then there's Doug, a tall, country Arkansas boy and Physics major who performs spoken word poetry in his free time. Go figure. They already had the prime locations for all their gear. But I'm pretty laid back, so it's cool. They seem all right enough. But I will say that Doug likes to cut the air off in the middle of the night—and in Houston, that will without fail lead to sweat city.

I am really wondering if computer engineering is the way to go for me, seeing as how I don't like math and science, ya know? All I do is play my Makaveli (Tupac), Ben Folds Five, and Radiohead CD's every night to drown out the noise of the door going in and out with their friends and guests . . . Ahh, good times.

Mama Dear calls me almost nightly, asking how I'm doing. You called a few times too, but I only got the messages. I will come over next weekend to see how y'all are in your new apartment. Heard you even had a car, too. Way to go, Mama.

On a completely unrelated side note—I am so tired of missing my *General Hospital.* Jonathan Jackson is the most talented young actor out there—in any medium. Lucky and Liz . . . magical. Well, honors English is calling my name, and this time, I have to answer.

Wish me luck,

- Manny

September 13, 1997

I caught the Metro Bus to Mama Dear's house this morning. Two weeks away at college and already running back home . . . And yes, she did my laundry for me. I'm not above admitting that. Saw y'all later on that day. I was pleasantly surprised that you found only a two-bedroom apartment for you and all the kids, but between rent and the car note, I understand. Looks like old Dante will be on that couch in the living room for a while . . .

It's an okay enough place, but there are some *characters* living over there. I just hope you are careful and keep a mindful eye on the kids so they don't get in any trouble.

DJ and I went to Price Buster's when he gave me a ride back home. The cashier girl rang up all my microwave meals and said, "Ooh, I can tell you don't have a girlfriend to cook for you." *Mortal embarrassment.* DJ must have laughed for an hour straight.

Not much of a cook, and just fine with it,

- Manny

September 19, 1997

Hung out today with a really nice and cute girl named Jennifer at school, and it's a pretty good story. I used to help with her philosophy homework. I had always wanted to talk to her, and she made it easy by talking to me one day a few weeks ago before class. I asked how she and her boyfriend (guy she always sat with) liked the class and they laughed. Turns out the dude sitting beside her was her brother. It's just that I always saw them together, so I of course made the assumption. He was really cool as well. They actually played in a band together where she played bass, I think, at little places like the Ice House or something—obviously spots my wallflower self has never seen.

Anyway, we all became friendly, and her brother dropped the class. She ended up missing a bunch of school days due to work and asked me to help her out. And over the course of maybe six weeks, I did. Then, I finally built up the courage, poured myself a cup of ambition (read chocolate milk), and told her today how adorable her bug eyes were, and that she reminded me of Kermit the Frog. True story.

She was mortified. I was shamed. I swear to God, at that very second, her *actual* boyfriend rolled up. He was the biggest, buffest T-Rex looking dude I had ever seen up close. He gave me the quick onceover—*Total Recall* style—determined that I was not a threat, and then he planted a HUGELY inappropriate kiss on her in full display of my shattered emotions. I asked if she was good for the day. She nodded, so I snaked out the back entrance on my belly, in cowardice.

October 3, 1997

Please don't get offended, but I've become fond of an analogy in which I compare you to a wayward puppy that has been rescued off the street. Now this puppy catches a break, being taken in by a boy who will try his best to love and protect it. However, the little dog won't stay—it's like the streets are calling her name at night. And by all rights, she should know better after a while, seeing as how she's been hit by cars, chased by children, and the like. But nevertheless, there she is, hopping the fence every single day at the same time, not content to stay in a truly loving environment. And even though the boy does his best to help her out by tracking her down, bringing her home, and cleaning her up, every now and then she will snip at your hand. She will do this not out of disrespect or anger, but because she's seen so much abuse and mistreatment that it's hard to distinguish between a helping hand and a harmful one at times. And there is also that undeniable call of freedom. Yet, showing remarkable perseverance, the boy shrugs it off, goes to bed, and comes to accept the fact that he'll probably have to do this routine all over again the very next night. The point is that this tale is basically as open-ended as can be. The boy isn't a hero or a fool; the dog isn't ungrateful or mean. They both are, who they are.

I found myself relaying this story today in the third session I had with a doctor I spoke with at UH today. I told him how you had been forcible committed several times, and had been diagnosed and showing paranoid schizophrenic traits for the better part of the 90's. We did not label it that initially, as we though, it was just 'Selita being Selita.'

You have started up again though. And between that, me in college now, a few weeks ago when the weight of this all became too much to bear, instead of going to my History class, I took a 20 min walk down the campus boulevard, to an area of the University I had never seen before. And that was the longest walk of my life, full of starts-and-stops, shame, second guessing, and near tears. I was headed over to the Psychological Services Center at UH. While flipping through the student handbook the night before, I had noticed that they offered counseling for students on a sliding scale basis. It was a long and fearful walk up the street to that building. I'm still uncertain as to what I expected or wanted them to do for me. What was my biggest fear on that day, you ask? That I would run into someone I knew from class or last semester's dorm that would recognize me and force me to account for my being there. What can I say? I'm no hero.

The sign-in clerk told me that they would assign me a counselor out of the pool of doctors on call there, as availability permitted. And one more thing, it wouldn't be so much a doctor as it would be a psych doctoral student. I drew Dr. Atchison and would become extremely thankful for that shortly thereafter. He was a kind and earnest man, and didn't seem to have a judgmental bone in his body. But he threw me when he said the department's policy is to tape all of the sessions. My first (and second) thoughts were that there would be a group of counselors, sitting round-table style, just cracking up at my poor life's worries. Or, perhaps they would sell them on the internet at www. grownasscrybabies.com. Yet, Dr. Atchison assured me that nothing of the sort would happen. He said that the tapes were mostly for review, and that he and the other doctoral candidates were being watched by their teachers/bosses so that they could gain constructive criticism on their therapy styles and could be certain they were leading the discussions down the right path. This would of course turn out to be true; my secrets would remain in the vault. Yet, here *I* am unlocking the door for you to see. Go figure.

We met once. Then once again. It soon turned from a happenstance affair to a twice weekly get-together that lapsed from one semester to another. But try as we did, we could not make heads or tails of my, or should I say our, *situation*. He encouraged, supported, and played the valiant role of compassionate-corporal sounding board unlike any other. He showed the utmost interest in the kids' wellbeing, gave me his home and cell phone numbers, but in the end—there was no help he could actually offer me where you were concerned. He told me that taking you to MHMR would yield a repeat performance unless you became violent. And, for an unbelievably long yet brief moment, I thought about trumping up a few charges along these lines.

Dr. Atchison felt I should try a support group for families of the mentally impaired (NAMI), explaining that maybe they could help further my understanding of 'the process' of coping/loving someone who is mentally ill (in that order). He felt that you were hostile to me because of the role reversal in our lives, and that maybe if I got the kids' money out of your hands (Social Security payments), you'd 'walk the line.' Yet, his main advice was for me to just hang in there. I mean, he saw the outward change from which my inward struggles were manifesting themselves—ecstatic when I met a new girl, sad when it inevitably didn't work out; my weight fluctuation roller coaster; after taking months to grow my hair into braids past my shoulders, how I was not literally pulling it out daily, strand by strand. Mama Dear always told me this was a 'nervous condition', and once again, she was correct. It's called Trichotillomania, and is listed as an actual psychological disorder where someone can't resist the urge to pull their hair out.

In no way can I even attempt to blame him for my failings. He has done a yeoman's job of trying to be a pillar of strength in my crumbling world. And my response to this friendship, my reaction to a man who chose to help a lost cause? Well, I walked out on him, naturally. I just upped and stopped going after our last meeting. I canceled my next session fifteen minutes before it began and consciously decided to never make another one. I'm ashamed of that. I really am ashamed. Even if he did not need it, Dr. Atchison *deserved* the courtesy of an explanation, the thoughtfulness of a goodbye. But neither of those reactions are my trademarks—and if I'm no good at something, I don't believe in pretending otherwise. Besides, even if I stayed in therapy forever and a day, he still never could have solved my problems for me. That's why they're called a crisis and not a cakewalk I suppose.

Have a good night's rest.

- Manny

November 27, 1997

Thanksgiving in the hood. Brought my computer down so I could do some work on my essays over the mini-break. Your apartment complex looks worse and worse every time I see it, I swear. And then there was the whole 'boyfriend' that was sprawled out across the bedroom floor when DJ and I got there. You got three young girls in the house, Selita, and this guy was bragging about how he did time in the penitentiary?! . . . Time's up, and I am pissed. Gloves are off. I don't care what issues you've got—you need to pull your stuff together for those kids' sake.

Mama Dear begged me to come stay with y'all over the break—and I caved. She's given me everything I've ever needed my whole life, but I must admit that lately, she asks a lot of me in return. "Go stay with them, buy them groceries, clean up their house," and so forth . . .

I want to be a good grandson who she can be proud of, but it really is hard sometimes. Then she tells me at the last second, the car company you went to wanted to refinance the Ford Escort you just bought, but you would not go down to handle the papers, so they took possession of it *and* kept your deposit money. Too late by the time I got there, past the free look period to get out of the contract with a return of deposit. Best I can do now is file a complaint with the Better Business Bureau.

FYI, yesterday I finally called that support group Dr. Atchison tipped me off to a while back. I figured If I was coming home to deal with you for the holidays, I could use all the reinforcements I could get. Not sure if you remember, it's called NAMI. Stands for the National Association of Mental Illness. They have groups for people who suffer the disease themselves, as well as support groups for the families of the affected.

The person on the phone was rather friendly. It was like eight locations on the list, so I just picked the one that I thought I could get too most easily. I drove there and waited outside for about five minutes for it to start. And then about ten minutes after it started. And then till it was over and people began to leave. I never steeped foot in the door.

I just couldn't do it. I don't care if they are all 'in the same boat as me.' Or that to my shock there were 'all kinds' of people there, black, white, fat, skinny . . . I just can't open up to others about this stuff. Not any of my school friends I've known for years. Not even girls I date and really like and who know something is troubling me and beg me to share.

They can swear up and down all day that, "They don't care what it is," and that, "They will be there for me" through it all. But I won't budge. It's easy to speak those words, tout your commitment, patience, and understanding, *from far away*. Let them get a good close peek and see where those concrete convictions go. I guess a lot of people would say I'm ashamed or embarrassed of you. But nah, I think I'm more ashamed and embarrassed of *me* and *my failure* to get you the help you need . . . And plus, a lot of this stuff I have to say is unbelievably personal and deals with your life, and that of others. And some of those stories and secrets I honestly don't think I have the right to tell . . .

But who knows? They meet every week (or is it every other?) And everyone knows I'm famous for changing my mind at the drop of a hat. Must be that Gemini in me . . .

- Manny

January 1, 1998

Happy New Year's! Mama Dear wants me to come out of the UH dorms and move in with you and the kids. I told her I just don't think I can do it. I am just fine with going to school and working a full job on the side, giving y'all money, and checking in from time to time. Why do I need to do *more*?

I mean, at some point, I have to start being responsible for myself, above all else. I just got away from home for the first time, and now she wants me to go right back? Nah., I love her to death, but I just don't see it happening. Besides, your kids are over at her house almost all the time anyway. They go to school from there, eat there. They are with you only some weekends at the most—when you're not too busy with one of your 'gentleman callers,' that is . . . Whatever.

This is me signing off,

- Manny

February 6, 1998

I borrowed Arleta's car and took Jamon to Pancho's (awesome Mexican restaurant) today as a thank you for helping me do some chores, and just to get him out of the house. They have a buffet system that's cafeteria style. You go through the line and pick up what you want. Then when you want additional items, they come to your table and pick it up for you and bring it back. How do they know you need more? There are tiny Mexican flags at the table that you raise and lower. *Genius*. Pure, unbridled genius. Long story longer, Jamon can put it away. He had two huge plates to start, then kept calling the waitress over time and again. Two more tacos, two more sopapillas, two more flautas. On the twentieth trip or so, she was like, "Just two?" He said extremely slowly, "Yes, just two," and held up two fingers in slow motion. She and I broke out laughing. The drama came at the end. I didn't have my wallet, and Jamon was always broke. We were going to have to make a run for it! Not our finest hour again, but hey, being poor should not be a crime, right? We sent the waitress away to pick up a huge amount of food on her next visit and we made our way to the soft serve yogurt section (which I always found weird in a Mexican restaurant) and then took off for the back-security exit once the coast was clear. There were double doors with security alarms, so it beeped super loudly when we went out, and the staff shouted at us to stop (probably because it was a pain to reset the alarm). We made it to the car and hit the gas.    Funny thing was, when I reached in for my keys, something fell out of my pocket—the receipt! We had been in so long—over two hours—and had eaten so much, talked and flirted with the waitress to no end, that we had forgotten one of the fundamentals of Pancho's: You pay at the *beginning* of the sit-down meal, not at the end! I had just enough cash to pay the bill up front, and that's why I had no change left over. When we realized we had dined and dashed on a meal that was already paid for, we couldn't stop laughing as if our lives depended on it, realizing we now have one more story we can always reminisce about . . .

- Manny

April 12, 1998

Giving myself a little early birthday present. I'm going back to see the psychologist at school today that was heling me last semester. Just to talk through some stuff. Had to admit to myself a few days back that with the pressure from school, Mama Dear asking me to leave the dorms, insane hours at work, and running back and forth to stay with you on weekends due to worrying about you and the kids because I'm not there to play the role of protector . . . it has gotten to be a tad much.

I had been thinking more and more about Dr. Atchison lately. He was as close to a friend as I had while at UH . . . College is weird. Especially the huge ones with 30k plus students like mine. You can borrow a pencil from someone, or see them in the gym, bump into them in the game room, and so forth. But if they're not in your major, your dorm, your extracurricular group or your frat house, then there's a good chance you'll never see them again once a class is over outside the odd library or Student center run-in. You can be as known, or as anonymous, to your heart's content as you desire.

Besides the occasional high school associate that I run into at the library or cafeteria, I have only hung out with maybe one person per semester at UH. Both guys are actually named James. One from the fall semester is so good on the basketball court that I begged him to try out at UH. He played on a South Texas high school team, and actually was able to walk-on in at UH this spring. He can thank me with some floor side seats if he makes it pro. The other James is my ping-pong arch-nemesis who I met in a gym class. Our friendship consists of basketball, racquetball, video games, and the odd on-campus free movie. This is how I keep all of my friendships, because the more involved they became, the wider the parameters, and the greater the scrutiny. I learned this in middle school after getting tired of the "Where is your dad, what's wrong with your mom, why don't y'all have a car?" type of questions.

A real friendship, a deep and lasting one would be nice. But if I am always self-alienating, pretending and hiding, I'm not sure how that could ever work . . . I guess I just really need someone to listen to me for a change—*as long as it may take.* Hence circling back to Dr. Atchison.

I really hope he is cool with me coming back, and not just feeling obligated like he has to because it's his job . . .

We soon shall see.

- Manny

May 23, 1998

Well, I think today will officially be the last time I ever call Dr. Atchison (the psychologist/psychiatrist from UH) outside of work, even though he repeatedly said I could for emergencies. Our sessions have been going well, and I never called him before, and thought it would be ok to do it just this once. But his wife picked up the phone, and (understandably) she did not sound thoroughly pleased to hear the sound of my voice. It was a dumb move on my part. I was feeling bad, and he offered the number way earlier, but still—short of a limb or something falling off, I should not have called him at *home*. I really mostly wanted to tell him I would probably skip our next session.

I've been doing that a lot lately. Ever since he told me point blank that he had no magic beans to sell me. Meaning, that is, that we're all in a tough spot, and it ain't going away with no end-all-to-be-all quick fix. Yeah, how dare he tell me the *truth*, right?

Oh well, got to go find something to get myself into. And by that, I of course mean falling to sleep watching reruns of *General Hospital* I taped earlier today.

Sonny Corinthos is so cool (and his pretty-boy enforcer Jason too). Luke and Laura, Lucky and Liz. The new Carly is growing on me too, but the O.G. Carly was *Legit* and will never be forgotten.

- Manny

June 21, 1998

Lordy, Lordy, look who's forty. Happy Birthday, Selita! And I don't care what anyone says—you don't look a day over thirty-nine. If I'm lying, I'm dying.

Well, your dutiful mother has finally done it. Mama Dear convinced me to terminate my housing contract for summer school, drop those classes, and come live with you and the kids from now on while I commute. I have no idea what I am getting myself into. I'll have to write the trust people and ask for some expense money . . . I'll tell them it's for my school expenses, so they shouldn't argue it—*too* much. Famous last words, right? Well, the first thing we need is a car, then a bigger apartment. I'm going to look at some places with Aunt Arleta today. I suppose this is really my childhood's end. I barely even knew thee . . .

- Manny

July 15, 1998

Benvenuto. That's either the Italian expression for 'hello', or 'give me some more frozen ice treats.' How should I know? I'm not a licensed phrenologist . . .

I had a real bad accident on I-45 earlier three days ago, as you *should* very well know, but will instead guess, you are not aware of. Didn't even have my first car that long at all. Some guy side-swiped me out of nowhere. Hmm, maybe it was a warning from the heavens to watch more closely where I'm going. Or to not make late night runs to McDonalds for burgers and shakes at closing time. Too close to call . . .

I hit the freeway barrier at about 50 mph, but walked away with only my faith in driving shattered and my left leg hurting a good bit. The only plus is that it was a cash car that I did not even have time to register in my name, a junker I got for $400 from this dude at the mechanics' shop. Mark VIII was the name of the model, I think. I left it there and flagged a ride down to a gas station where I called a cab.

I think I will check that car lot on North Shepherd Drive, the one close to the Park-and-Ride Arleta used to ride to work at the Medical Center, and get a nicer car this time. Although with the nightmares I've been experiencing lately, I don't really think I'll be driving it for a while. I'm talking dreams of me getting slammed at full-on impact and coughing up blood as I valiantly try to claw my way out of the jammed door, just as the car begins to ignite into an inferno. Yeah, nothing but tossing and turning for me for the foreseeable future . . .

I am pretty convinced that I will die behind the wheel. No joke. I am an iffy driver to begin with—started way late (seventeen and a half—I must be the only child in the world who begged relatives *not* to let him drive). I get nervous, and I am not good with quick reflexes. That's a deadly trifecta right there. Now I'm off to search for a monthly bus pass at Kroger.

- Manny

September 16, 1998

Steph's birthday is next week, which means of course I'll run out to get her a cake, ice-cream, and no doubt a gift she'll truly resent me for. Fun times indeed.

Thanks for washing my clothes for me when I got them caked in mud this morning. But no thanks at laughing at me with reckless glee. Promise that's the second-to-last time I will try to jump over a concrete parking barrier in the pouring rain . . . Another life lesson well learned by yours truly. 'The more you know'—and cue NBC rainbow colored shooting star.

You were pretty civil about the whole affair. I wish we had more chats like that, Selita, I really do. That would be preferred to me coming home to you throwing a tirade and then me running straight to my room for refuge, and to cut on my music as I pretend that I am thankful for the life I lead . . .

I guess we're doing okay for the most part. We have a nice three-bedroom apartment on the border of FM 1960. The kids are in really good schools, I got us a Chevy Lumina, only six years old with low miles, and it fits our huge clan. And though everyone in the family is slapping me on the back and saying what a great job I'm doing and how responsible I am . . . I just feel . . . *empty*.

Because I'm dying inside. I can easily see this being my routine for the next twenty years if I allow it to be. Especially if Mama Dear lives to a nice old age to grind me down about it (though of course I want her here forever – even if it means nagging me to my death).

It's just that all the stuff I've done has been cosmetic and, on the surface. But the big things—those I have *no clue* how to tackle—remain. Like your schizophrenia, your mood swings, your depression, your diabetes, and getting you to go to the doctor and taking your medication regularly; and the kids asking, "why their daddy had to die and if I will be there new daddy . . . Because we sure do need one." What am I possibly supposed to say to *that*?

I go to school, and work. And then back to home to begin anew. And though at home there are five people constantly near me, at work there are fifty, and at school there are tens of thousands—yet I always feel *alone*. I can't reach out and touch anyone I know that has a situation even remotely close to mine. I hear them in the recreation center talking about clubs and restaurants while I'm thinking about bills and elementary homework assignments. I lost contact—intentionally—with all my friends from high school because I talked such a good game about 'making it big' and going into advertising and writing movies. Yet, here I am . . . living with my family, sleeping on a bunk bed with my little bro on Spiderman sheets, and barely scraping by day-to-day.

I saw the saddest video ever by this group named Green Day, and it somewhat dealt with this same issue. It was called "Time of your Life" and instead of having fun and doing cool things, kids were working, cleaning up, having miserable times in their young adult lives.

I ain't digging ditches over here, so I'm sorry if this whiny rant is irking you. It's just that I so want you to get better—as of ten years ago. Because then, maybe *I* could get better, too. A little bit at a time.

What a pair we make.

- Manny

❦

September 23, 1998

Steph turned twelve yesterday, FYI. My psychology professor asked us what our greatest dreams and aspirations were. I mentioned something along the lines of becoming a commercial director for Nike, but that was not even in my top ten in reality.

What I truthfully want is to get you some help. And I know even if that happened, it wouldn't mean that we would have a perfect familial relationship by any means. You would more or less revert to your *old* personality, which I never was a huge fan of to begin with. But you'd be better. And that's what matters—to all of your family.

You could watch your kids come into adolescence, then adulthood. Have more than a moment's peace, a good night's rest. There would be no more looking for 'spies' or accusing strangers of 'reading your thoughts' and 'plotting against you.' God knows, I've long given up the notion of you waking up 'fixed' one morning with the turmoil of our past way in the rear view. I have no delusions—as I did in my youth—of you profusely thanking me, or even saying, "Good job, Manny." Or, "Way to hold down the fort while I was *gone*." I'm not doing this for any great prize at the end of the road. And it's not as if I'm some kind of saint; oh no, far from it. It's just that I now realize that you didn't bring this upon yourself. You didn't ask for your mind to be decimated and your spirit to be vanquished. You didn't fall apart in order to make me take care of the family. And I would ask that you please forgive me, as I've made more than my share of mistakes. But I've recently made my share of realizations. at the top of that list is that getting you better is not a chore or task, but an *calling*. I owe it to you, my brother and sisters, and myself as well. Whenever I occasionally lose sight of this, I recall what Mama Dear used to tell me. She'd say, "Manny, you know the right thing to do, and you know you got to live with *you*."

I also never want for positive reinforcement from others. Family members and my doc go out of their way to tell me how proud they are of me, that they are impressed by the responsibility I've taken on at such a young age, and of my own volition. But a part of me wonders—do they just say that so I'll keep in the role assigned and not try to shift my burden on to *them*?

As I said, compliments are not what I'm all about. But you know what? Sometimes, when the money's low and the bills are high, and I want to laugh but instead I cry—then these well wishes sure can come in handy. Man, that sounds like a country song right there.

Mama Dear likes to tell me how, "The Lord 'doesn't give us any more than we can handle." So maybe I should feel pride in the fact that God saw fit to put so much on my plate, confident that I could bear the load. A spiritual vote of confidence in the cosmic boardroom, if you will. Perhaps one day I will look back at my battle scars with pride, knowing that I indeed earned them . . .

Remember how I once told you when I was fifteen, I told Mama Dear that I wished I was a 'normal' kid and did not care so much about other people's pain. Well I won't lie (not that I have anything against lying; it's a great way to pass the time), every now and then I question if she was actually correct in her assessment of me. That me being this way does actually make a difference. I ask myself what a more carefree me would be like, if I did not take things so close to heart. But I realize that early on in my life I was up for that role—I just didn't get the part.

- Manny

November 24, 1998

The Lord shines on me today. Tupac's greatest hits album came out and I raced to Blockbuster to get it . . .

I never thought he could keep topping himself. From "Keep Ya Head Up," to "Dear Mama," to "I Ain't Mad at Cha," and "Life Goes On" . . . But he has done it . . . I swear, song # 9 on Disc 1, "Unconditional Love," is the greatest song in the history of the world.

His lyrics are magic, and his flow is *the truth*, and . . . Man, I know you've heard me bumping it in my room from here to infinity all night, right? Well, that's where I'm back to now.

"How come I never made it? Maybe it's the way I played it . . ."

- Manny

December 16, 1998

I was just thinking about how Mama Dear laughs every time she sees the actress Jackée on television. You know, the one from that show *227* back in the day, and then "Sister, Sister" more recently? She never misses an opportunity to remind me of how, when I was six or seven years old, I always used to say that I was going to run off to Hawaii to live with Jackée. Mama Dear claims that when she asked me what I would do with Jackée in Hawaii, my answer was quite direct—*make love*. Oh boy. I will never live that down. This cracks her up no end whenever she spots her in reruns. She'll notice that I get embarrassed and then she'll back off. I'll let a smile creep out, and she'll put her arm around me and say she's sorry, and everything is just fine. That's my granny.

Mama Dear is fond of saying that, "God will reward my patience," and that I "Already have my crown waiting on me in heaven—all I have to do is pick it out once I get there." Well, one time I asked her if I could get a pawn loan on my heavenly reward, since I'm struggling pretty bad on earth. And though she didn't really understand my joke (or she did and just felt it bombed), she smiled politely and said, "Nah, honey. The Lord don't work that way."

Quite a different response from when I used to tell you jokes, and you said that, "If I had time to play then I had time to study." You ran a tight ship, Selita. A tight ship indeed. When you were around and not out chasing men, that is . . .

But I digress. Back to the subject at hand. I am in a storytelling kind of mood, and I would like to fill you in and refresh your memory a bit about my beloved grandmother, your mother, Mrs. Mama Dear.

Mama Dear was born Vivian Odessa Glaze on January 23, 1925. Her mother, Mama Alma, was one-fourth Cherokee. Mama Alma had a sister named Minnie who loved to fight *and* drink, so the stories go. Mama Dear says that whenever Gussie—Mama Dear's grandmother—would hear an ambulance in the street, she would tell Alma, "Go see about Minnie." To which Alma invariably replied, "I can't do nothing with Sister . . ."

Gussie was half-Cherokee, and her brother Charlie apparently ran a numbers lottery in his day. Gussie's mother, Mama Dear's great-grandmother, Ms. Dinah was full-Cherokee (I saw a pictures of her with the headdress, but can't be sure if she was Cherokee. Any black person mixed with Native American had that designation it seems, no matter what tribe their people may have actually belonged to.). There used to be a huge life-like portrait of Dinah in Janet's house that frightened Little Greg. Everyone, including Little Greg himself, says that Ms. Dinah's picture scared the living daylights out of him, and he would run away crying every time he saw it.

All these women shared the trademark Native American looks of high cheekbones and long wavy hair, just like Mama and Rosalind have. They used to call Mama Dear 'Baby Glaze' in high school. I know this because Rosalind went with Mama to their fifty-year reunion and ran into every man in her grade who said he was in love with her in school.

They said that Mama Dear, "Was so fine that she would have Mae West ask what was really going on!" Mama Dear had two sisters and one half-brother, and all three preceded her in death. They were

Muggins (the oldest), Aunt Erma, and Uncle Pretty Boy (Matthew, the youngest). I never met Pretty Boy, but I hear he was an amalgamation of your brother June Bug and your nephew Little Greg (Janet's boy). Good-looking, charismatic, a veteran, and extremely smart. And with all those traits going for him, he still drank himself to death in his early forties . . .

You used to give me a hard time when I was younger for spending so much time with Mama Dear. You told me how she was so 'horrible' to you when you were a child, never gave you any attention, and so forth. And, of course, these are many of the same things I've said about you to Mama Dear. Funny how some things come full circle, huh? Anyway, Mama Dear grew up extremely poor, but she was exceptionally smart. As a child, I always wondered why she had fake teeth, and one day she explained to me that when she was eighteen or so, she was in a terrible car wreck and went through the windshield. As a result, she lost nearly all of her teeth, had the remainder pulled out, and has worn dentures ever since. It also left her with a lifetime fear of driving, and she has never gotten behind the wheel to this day (except for one trip to San Francisco with your daddy, James L., when he tried to teach her in the '70s, but that did not go well given all the insane hills and busy traffic up there).

Janet is the second oldest of Mama's kids (after Arleta). You have had a really strained relationship with her and Rosalind because of their trying to help out during the court case with Ray, and leading the charge to have you committed where you were at your worst. And though I'm getting ahead of myself here, it must be said that I never could fully repay them for all that they have done for us over the years, but I surely will try.

Anyhow, Janet said that Mama's family felt that she married "beneath" her station when she fell in love with James L. He was charming, tall, and a playboy in *every* sense of the word. He was from the South side of Houston and worked for decades as a sanitation worker. He was viewed as unacceptable by Mama's family for several reasons: For one, he didn't have her level of education. She had a nursing degree while he worked with his hands. He was also extremely dark of skin, while she is very light in appearance, with the aforementioned high cheekbones and wavy hair. He moved them out to the 'boondocks' of Acres Homes where they had no indoor plumbing and drank 'well water' as opposed to that from the city. He had a second job as a repairman, so the front yard was littered with spare parts from numerous televisions and radios in various stages of completion. They also farmed in the early years, so there was the occasional chicken and goat wandering throughout the property. I suppose what followed should have been expected. This included being derided by her family, the neighbors, and even her neighbors who were family. Everyone's a critic.

But Mama Dear never let it bother her. She always kept her head about her, Rudyard-Kipling style. She said there, "Ain't no shame in being poor," even as she had her own blood snub their noses at her, refusing to visit, etc. I'll tell you what though, if you ever see a more gracious woman standing in a free food line, it'll be a shock to me. Been there with her at church donation centers, and have seen that firsthand.

Many of my cousins say Mama Dear always treated me as her favorite. And you know what, all your sisters say she treated you the same way, Selita. While I never saw anything but kindness and the like, I'm told that this was the '*New Testament*' version of my grandmother. Apparently, back in the day, she was known to raise a little hell and get mighty rambunctious with y'all. I'm hearing extension cord whooping's that followed warm baths so the skin would be *nice and supple*. Whoa. I must say, I'm glad I never had the pleasure. Just a branch/switch whooping or 2 at most that I can recall.

And like most of us, she mellowed considerably as life, and its ensuing disappointments, lingered on. And her family was always there to remind her of her status. Although they worked no harder than Mama, by marrying 'appropriately' and limiting their number of offspring, they had considerably more success than her. Now I can't speak at all on Pretty Boy, and I only vaguely remember Muggins. But Aunt Erma, a.k.a. Diggy, is someone I have gotten to know quite well since we connected at the reunion. I go to visit her, take her to the store, take Mama over to see her every now and then, and so forth.

Remember how I told you that she and Mama Dear stayed about five minutes apart, yet hardly saw each other? They preferred to talk several times a day on the phone. This was at first out of convenience, and then later it was due to necessity when Aunt Erma suffered the first of several strokes and could no longer get around with ease.

Now when I was younger, we hardly ever traveled to Aunt Erma's house. Most of my aunts and cousins refused to go, citing the way she talked to people. Her humor was a tad *caustic*, to say the least. She said at the reunion after going several years without seeing me, "Ooh Manny, I'm so glad you grew, I sure do hate a short man." I could have *died* laughing. Now whereas others took offense, I saw it for what it was—Diggy is just *cold blooded*.

My motto is that I don't look for the best in people, I look for the *worst*, and if I can handle that, then everything else is gravy. Two quick things you need to realize about Aunt Erma—the first being she fronted me the $120 for a Kaplan SAT prep course. I initially wanted to spend it on a greater good—the latest Air Jordan's (fabulously trendy yet insanely overpriced sneakers). Mama Dear, in her infinite wisdom, would not allow me to. My score improved from 1180 to 1320, and I was offered multiple scholarships. Good looking-out, old girl.

Also, like you with Stephanie's dad, Arthur Lee, Erma shot an abusive spouse. Unlike you, she killed him dead on the spot. She admitted it to the police, and did not duck and dodge the blame, trying to explain it away that she did it because he was hurting her children. That was the story you told Selita, and even though I knew better, I remained silent, because you were fighting for your life to stay out of prison. And besides, he was in fact abusive in beating you. And a crime against my mother, is all in all, a crime against *me* as well. Anyhow, I try to visit her every now and then—partly because I like her, but mostly because I know Mama Dear would appreciate it because so few others do.

Back to Mama Dear. As I said, she did what she could with what she had, and I never felt unloved or lesser than because we went without, as long as I had her near me. I can recall one Christmas in 1985 where to eat we only had toast, jelly, and grits over the entire two-week school break. But it was just me and her (Steph and the others kids did not exist yet), and I could not have been happier.

I later found out she had so little because her husband, as I alluded to before, was a real 'man about town.' Different cars, different houses, even an entirely different family . . . When he passed in April 1987, a good deal of money was unaccounted for. It all came to a head at his funeral, where the majority of his grieving children were apparently not born to Mama Dear. Now you gotta remember that, right Selita? There was an entirely different family collective in attendance. While one mildly resembled Rosalind, another was the spitting image of June Bug . All hell almost broke out when they went to view the body, but at the age of eight, I merely chalked it up to commonplace funeral activities.

Another tragic side note is when I found out the truth about Clay. You know, your boyfriend before Ray and Arthur Lee, for the first six or so years of my life. He was super nice, crazy about both of us, loved

Prince, and had a drip-drip Jheri Curl *to die for*. He worked (then and now) as a sacker at a Kroger's grocery store, and he loved you to death. But for some (or many) reasons, you just didn't want him. When you broke it off, it destroyed him. However, I later found that you did not have much of a choice. It seems that James L. used to 'know' Clay's mom, and there was a chance he could have been your half-brother. Man, I thought only pretty *white people* had those kinds of melodramatic, soap-opera type problems . . .

At one point, I'm extremely ashamed to admit, I believed that people 'like you' neither needed nor deserved children. This meant people with psychological, financial, or emotional issues of any type. But I've long since realized my error, and I'm here to apologize for those sentiments. Certain people are less equipped to be successful parents than others; that, is just a *fact*. However, everyone has the God-given *right* to try to extend (and better) themselves through the life and love of a child. And even more importantly, I feel that for each parent who lags behind in their duties, there will always be a Mama Dear-type who is potentially there to pick up the slack. I've seen it in the trailer parks not far from where we lived with white families, in the barrios with Mexican friends, and later with Middle Eastern kids I have met in high school and college, where they have several generations under one roof, raising kids collectively, and helping each other through the process.

I can remember Granny and I arguing only two times in my entire life. I already mentioned the first incident. The second happened yesterday, and was about Jamon (your nephew), when she told me to kick him out of our apartment because he was no good, used marijuana, etc. I asked her why, if she did not kick out her own crack-fiend son (June Bug, Jamon's daddy), should I be expected to do it to my weed-smoking cousin? She replied, "It's impossible trying to tell someone who knows everything anything at all." To which I replied, "That's why you don't ever hear me asking for advice." I then stormed out of her house. Not the brightest and most shining moment in the history of loving grandsons, to say the least.

I will confess that I have come to feel in time that Mama has helped me out all these years not because she truly *loved me*, but because she felt *sorry* for me. Since you were blessed with so much in life Selita—looks, brains, humor—and you *still* ended up with your mind lost, she feels it must be *her* fault. She deems it her responsibility, and failure, for you not succeeding in life. Therefore, she's been making up for it all of these years, in my humble opinion, by trying not to make the same mistakes with me. She hasn't poured all of this love and attention into me because I'm Manny—unique and deserving of love. It's because I'm Manny—Selita's son. Or Manny—a boy to bring up right as opposed to June Bug . She laid the groundwork years ago so I would simultaneously stay clear of your respective paths, and yet still have the compassion in me to care enough to change your lot in life. That would be my repayment to her—continuing her mission of helping take care of you, thus breaking the chain of guilt that has seemingly forever weighed on her weary soul. And in no way am I saying that this was a monstrous thing to do. It's just not something the grandmother I know and love would ever attempt—consciously or otherwise.

I've wanted to ask her so many times over the years if my theory was true. Just wake up and drive over to her house, ring the bell, and ask has she stood behind me all these years out of love, or *obligation*. Was it because I earned her compassion, or because she felt I could never get it elsewhere? Every time she asks me over the phone to recap what happened on *General Hospital* that day (if she accidentally fell asleep and missed it), I want to blurt it out. I'm just dying to know.

But I'll never ask. Not out of respect—which is how it should be—but due to *fear* of the answer I would receive. Which is a validation in itself I suppose, that I already know in my heart what her response would be . . .

I think I mentioned this before, how Janet or Mama came across a copy of the deposition where you sued Hermann Hospital for their negligence and how it led to my scars. Mama Dear told the lawyers of my school situation—the teasing, fights, etc. She said that I often ran home crying, asking why God would be punishing me. She remarked that I was, "Lucky to be alive." For the longest time, I felt this was pure insanity. Lucky?! I should consider myself lucky?

But sometimes, when the home front is calm, you're quiet, and the kids are laughing, I reconsider it all. On those rare days when I'm not stressed out, because I got a decent grade in school, or they're running a *Duck Tales* marathon on the cartoon channel, I can somewhat see what Mama Dear meant. At these precious times, I guess I am a little lucky after all.

Whenever I am away and don't visit her for a while, I find myself missing Mama for all the wrong reasons. How she made me feel about myself is high on the list. How she gave me tremendous love as a child when no one else could/would—not even you. How she made this sad little boy think a withered old lady would slay a dragon if it meant keeping him from harm.

On those days I ran home crying, I was not aware of anything offhand that I had done wrong to deserve a treatment of this caliber from society. And Mama Dear would often cry silently too. She would then try to get me to understand that I was normal, like any other child. The only difference I had was actually on the *inside*. That's what made me special. That's what made me different—not the burns on my head. But I was usually not appeased, and I would beg her to tell me when it would get better. When would people see my inside instead of my outside—just like she could? And her reply was always the same, "Sooner than you think, honey. Sooner than you think."

- Manny

January 11, 1999

I did some super serious research today on depression. There is supposed to be like a really cool study going on right now at Baylor College of Medicine down in the Medical Center. However, they clearly made note that if the patient presents characteristics of schizophrenia as well that they are *not eligible* for the program.

So much for that. But hey, maybe I should lie to try and get you in anyway? I would more than settle on them working out the depression and bipolar tendencies and leaving the schizophrenia for another day.

"Two out of three ain't bad."

- Manny

January 11, 1999 May 3, 1999

May 3, 1999

Cheyenne is being held back in school. Her first-grade teacher is tripping. Saying she's so bad off that not even summer school will be enough to help her get caught up in math. How the hell does she know that?! I didn't see a crystal ball on her desk when I went there today.

I brought Janet along for support, but that damn teacher wouldn't budge. The truth is, I feel terrible for letting that kid down. She reads so well, has a great personality and vocabulary. I just figured her math would pick up eventually. I just knew it would.

One day I came home and could not believe I saw you giving her the *wrong* answers on simple addition and subtraction problems. Not on purpose, but still . . . Your brain is so off kilter that something basic like that escaped you. And if that's been going on all year . . .

God forgive me please.

- Manny

September 12, 1999

I've been working with Cheyenne since May on her Math, and she has a B+ average now this new school year. . . Okay, I will tell everyone else in the family I brought her up to an 'A,' but that's my poetic license, right?

We go through math routines like something straight out of the *Rocky* movies. I even put on sweatbands and bandanas sometimes while cranking my '80s CDs—swear to God.

- Manny

October 21, 1999

Something's gotta give Selita—and I promise it *won't* be me. I'm so damn *tired* of people making excuses for you. "Oh, she's sick. Oh, it's postpartum. Oh, she's led a hard life." Well, who the hell hasn't? People can look at my battle-scarred face at twenty years old and tell I ain't had a life filled with ice cream and unicorns.

I can't believe you went into that leasing office *again*, after I told you not to. They will *Kick Us Out* of our home if you go up there with your antics again . . . Talking about how people are following you and how unsafe you feel and . . . Ahhh!

I don't need you to thank me or be appreciative, but I will not stand for you *sabotaging* me and making this situation as difficult as possible for me.

That just ain't right. And sick or not, you know it.

- Manny

October 28, 1999

My Psychology class is the *worst*. It's always crowded to the max, the teacher thinks he's the second coming of Don Rickles with his put-downs.

It's not all that bad—but terribly close. We do occasionally talk about some interesting subjects. Take today for instance, when our lecture centered on natural instinct. How racism, or shall I say self-segregation, is programmed into our genetic makeup. People simply tend to migrate toward their own, from preschool children on the playground to burly ball players on the football field. Sure, they will undoubtedly show respect (to a degree) to others, but they will feel most comfortable playing and hanging out with others whose appearance mirrors their own.

This naturally occurring phenomenon left me quite the dilemma growing up. I was black, yet I looked Hispanic or Puerto Rican. African Americans thought I was mixed, and since I naturally denied it, they took me for a liar. Hispanics thought me a sell-out fraud when I 'deserted my heritage,' since I not only looked like them, but had a Hispanic-sounding name as well. And with my scars, kids didn't have a lot of incentive to give me a second shot once we got off on the wrong foot. Throw in that I was short, bespectacled, and overweight, and well, you can pretty much see that I hit the loser lottery. It took a special kind of person to befriend someone such as myself back in the day. To reach out to a boy who no one thought was worth the effort. And although I have not kept in close contact with any of them, I continue to remember and appreciate them to this day.

I was also unable to help my own cause (a phrase for pitchers who get a hit in baseball that is both overused and undervalued) growing up in the ghetto. As you well know, the kids around those parts play mighty rough, yet their cruelty was right on par with my better-off classmates at Catholic grade school where I was always an outcast.

And though I had it pretty rough with the neighborhood hard-heads, I wasn't on my own. Dreis (Arleta's boy) stood up for me many a day. And this is quite remarkable in hindsight, considering how he was picked on as a child for being a 'sissy.' And maybe those bullies weren't completely ignorant, because Dreis did eventually admit that he was gay in his twenties. But I'll tell you what—I could care less—because everyone deserves love and to be happy for who and what they are. AND that 'sissy' kicked a lot of butt on my behalf!

So not having 1980s era Michael Jackson-type popularity in the hood, I tended to stay in the house. I guess I would have been considered a latchkey kid, except I didn't have the required key. Or a necklace to hang it from.

Most of the time, there was always an array of cousins and aunts residing there—moving out during the good times, moving in during the bad. Our sleeping arrangements changed more often than the Clippers' starting lineup from week to week. You'd never know who would get the couch in the front room or den, if there would be two or four kids in Mama Dear's bed (lying horizontal or vertical), etc. Yet with all this uncertainty, I always knew I would have one constant companion who'd never leave me—the television!

Today's conventional wisdom suggests only 'bad' parents allow their children to watch TV all day. Well, I would argue that it's neither irresponsible nor lazy. How about those 'attentive' parents who give their kids permission to stay out of the house for hours on end, giving them the opportunity to raise all kinds of hell. And I know that many of the adults who grew up lonely as I did love to gripe and moan about how they were left at the house, with nothing to do . . . Well boo freaking hoo. I was at home because Mama Dear was working sixty, count 'em, *sixty* hours a week to provide for a household of children she was in no way whatsoever obligated to.

Anyway, my fascination with television coupled with my constant exposure to classically trained bullies left me inside all the time. Due to my sensitivity concerning my looks, I was what you often referred to as 'babied' by your mother. Whenever Mama brought toys for the kids, I got the best; if she brought donuts home, I got the first. Speaking of donuts, Dreis still holds it against me an infamous incident when she brought back two Shipley glazed donuts after her shift one night. I ate mine, and then I licked his entire donut before he could get to it, in the hopes it would gross him out and he would let me have it. He popped me, I told, and Mama Dear wore him out proper—like with a glorious, old-timey, behind the shed whooping. And though I diabolically reveled in it at the time, as I look back upon the scenario now . . . I still pretty much revel in it. See, Selita, I'm not here to lie, and this is proof to you that I'm not a great guy. I'm a grown man who's made a lot of mistakes . . .

But the kid gloves Mama (and you) used on me did not come without their price. I could not go out alone, or even spend the night at my relatives' houses till I was almost twelve. I could not walk home from school, and only when I turned sixteen and went on a recruiting trip to Texas A&M did I stay overnight with friends. In addition, I was the victim of my Uncle Jun June Bug's previous mistakes. As you know, he used to be 'The Man' back in the day—smart, handsome, and so forth. But he tried to be a thug, which was not his forte at all. He tried to roll with the big dogs, but, unfortunately, they chewed him up and spit him out. He has been beaten, shot, and jailed numerous times. He experienced kidney failure, alcoholism, gambling and crack addiction—you name it. One of my most vivid memories as a youth is of him cursing me out at eight years old, full as a tick with whiskey, telling me how, "Selita's a failure," and I'd "certainly be one too—so why even try"? Good times.

And then there's the time when I was twelve and I helped clean his wounds after he had been beaten following a session where he mouthed off to the law. Jimmy, Junior, James Jr., June Bug, he has so many names—just like the Devil, so many names. Yet like the true great villains of our day, he's also extremely complex. At times, he's capable of being as sweet as pie, helpful, charming as all get out. At other times, he shows a heart in which the light dares not enter, lest it be consumed. He could take you to a ball game, then pawn your beloved Nintendo for drug money; show you how to ride a bike, then curse at his mother like a dog in the street.

I've gone entire years without speaking to him. This is not even including the incident with Jamon previously mentioned. When I gave him the silent treatment, he'd change his tune. After a day or so when he was no longer 'full,' he'd realize the enormity of his actions and try to atone. All it took for poor Mama Dear would cave instantly, but he could kiss my butt from here to across the street, and I'd have none of it.

Even with all that, from this man came one of the people I have cared dearly for in the world—my cousin Jamon, who many fear is already too far down the same path as his dad. I wonder what created that storm inside of June Bug. What if he wasn't the only son to a house full of women, and he had an older brother to show him the ropes? What if his father had spent more time with him, and less time running the streets and chasing women? Would a better example at home have made him not look to emulate that hustler's life? You just don't know, but I honestly think it would have played out different, and his life could have been so much more . . .

- Manny

November 12, 1999

Yesterday was Dante's Birthday. He turned eight. We had cake. To make a short story even shorter—the end. Now let's talk about something far more interesting. Lets' talk about you for a change. Miss James Selita. That's the name of my burden; the name of my cross. Just kidding. Not really though. I've answered so many questions about your name, I feel as if I have more of a connection to it than my own. The initial response is always the same, "Why does your mom has a boy's name?" By now I truly wish I did not know the answer: Because you had a twin brother who was stillborn (just like Aunt Lynell), and when he passed, you were given his first name so he would be remembered.

You were the lightest of all of Mama Dear's children. 'Dirty Red' is what they called you. Some might say that you were the smartest too; but a revisionist looks at history would put that theory in jeopardy. It's been said that you played all the angles, that Mama Dear was 'color struck' at that point in time, showing favoritism to her lighter kids and grandkids. This is why you, then me, and later on Cheyenne have been bestowed with said 'favorite' title.

I've heard from your sisters that your mastery in the art of 'bitch-craft' (their words not mine) manifested very early on in life. Lying, sneaking out, going around with boys, putting on airs, talking down to people, escalating the Middle East crisis, and so forth. Now this did come from your sisters (and often time siblings are the worst, am I right?), so it should probably be taken with a cauldron of salt. But all in all, it sounds like the probable adolescent behavior of the Selita I've known all these years.

Yet, as with each of us, there's much more to you than meets the eye. There's a different portrait of you painted by my older cousins. Before your illness, they remember you as the life of the party, always with a smile on your face and a drink in your hand. Little Greg remembers that you were quick to wrestle any girl or boy, and you loved to pull out your 'sneak suplex' on unsuspecting victims. He also told me how you were such a terrible driver, you decided to wear a pair of 'Daisy Dukes' to your exam to give the instructor a little extra incentive to pass you. I'm not even gonna attempt to speculate on that one . . .

D.J. (Aunt Olivia's Boy) tells me how y'all used to team up to beat everyone in dominoes and spades, going by the moniker of 'The James Gang' (James Selita, D.J., James Jr. aka June Bug), as you talked trash to your opponents the entire time. No lectures here, because I myself am a terrible loser, and even worse winner—like mother, like son . . . And on the serious side, helping Brit (D.J.'s sister) gets her first job, doing her resume, buying her a business suit, and so on. And back to my main man—Little Greg. He tells me you cosigned for his first apartment when he moved to Austin, helped with his bills, and even wrote a term paper or two for him in English at The University of Texas.

Little Greg is my real-life hero. Now to begin with, I must say that his name is rather ridiculous. He's called Little Greg because

Rosalind married 'Big Greg' (pretty good guy, my basketball mentor and foil) many years ago, and so they used 'Little Greg' for my cousin as to not cause confusion when talking about either of the Greg's. However, Little Greg is close to forty, so to say that moniker is a little dated rings extremely true. Now, in the grand scheme of things, I look to Pac and Malcolm for my inspiration. But for a real-life soul to be my Bible, I look toward Greg. Since we're both nerdy, chubby, wear crooked glasses, and were quiet and sheltered growing up, most everybody over the years say that I remind them of him. I personally take that as the highest accomplishment they could bestow upon me. Neither of us smoke or drink. And whereas I consider myself to be pretty smart, Greg on the other hand is *devastatingly brilliant.* But like yours truly, he's had some real testing moments, and near misses with greatness. From never being acknowledged by his father, to losing out on a full ride scholarship to Texas A&M, to meeting racists professors at UT upon enrolling there, or finding what seemed to be the girl of his dreams only to have her turn psycho/stalkerish on him down the line . . . There is not a nicer, smarter guy in the world.

He's thirteen years older than me, and has been in Austin for most of my memory, so I did not have the privilege of growing up with him. But the times we did spend together—from him showing me this newfangled invention called the 'internet' in the mid-90s (when it was nothing more than bulletin board pages and 2-D images, to us going bowling, or seeing the *Teenage Mutant Ninja Turtles 2* movie (Ninja, Ninja Rap)—are some of my greatest memories. He is more or less my litmus test on life, because if he can pull out a victory with all that he's been through, then maybe, just maybe, I could one day too . . .

Suffice it to say, Greg's version of you doesn't quite sound like the mother I'm familiar with. Maybe the loud and boisterous part, because I've been known to get a tad verbose on the few happy days that roll my way. But the rest, you've got some explaining to do, missy. Where was this great hospitality at in my youth? For instance, when you *never* asked how my day was. Or this fabled generosity of which they speak? I recall you making me buy you a new pair of white shoes out of my birthday money when I accidentally spilled chocolate milk on your old ones. How about that kindness? Where was it when I brought home a 'B' in Pre-Algebra? I was expecting to hear, "You'll get 'em next time." But instead heard, "Bring it up to an A!" Could this possibly be the same lady who would constantly yell at me for dropping dishes, and then when I said sorry, would shake my shoulders till I would tear up, and whisper to me with devastating effect, "Don't be sorry. *Be better.*"

Now *that's* the Selita I know. Not the one my cousins appear to remember—but I wish it was. Maybe then I could tell the kids some great stories along the lines of those previously mentioned. Then they could know that you're capable of being happy, possibly being whole, and perhaps being more than they have seen. But you want to know a secret? I'm going to tell them those things anyway. Because they *did* happen, and someone did experience it, just not me. Why shouldn't those who matter the most—your children—have the same opportunity? It's not as if I'm making anything up or putting fairy tales in their heads. Besides, just like with Uncle Junior, I can't help but wonder, what really happened to you growing up. Who hurt you, disappointed you, enraged you – to mold the person that you became? Where did that laughter, joy, and free spirit go that everyone recalls you by? And more importantly, how do I get it back inside you, before it's too late?

One night, a few years back, Aunt Olivia sat with me in the den and told me some things concerning you that I had never heard before. They also dealt with me, and my so-called father. When I was a kid, Brit got mad at me once when I made some smart aleck remark along the lines of, "Be careful on your date—an unplanned pregnancy is a real mood killer." I was about ten when I said this, and she didn't miss a beat with her reply, "Yeah, I already know, because that's how you were born." *Ouch*. And the champ is down.

But in all reality, what was the big shock in hearing that I was unplanned? Oh no, my delicate ears. Okay, so I was a 'mistake.' Yeah, me and five million other black kids. Now back to me and Olivia. She went a little deeper than Brit that night in relaying to me my origin story. At first, she insisted he was an Iranian man named Habib. It appears you befriended one at Texas Southern while attending, which Mama Dear later verified. Olivia said this explains my 'off' looking skin color, bushy eyebrows, and world-class temper. Pretty funny stuff.

Then she got serious and told me his name was Manny as well. She says that she and D.J. met him one night, that he was short, right around my listed height of 5'8," had a very light skin tone. Frenchman or Creole they say, as most black people out of Louisiana are designated. D.J. also threw in that he had the biggest afro the world has ever seen—that it could possibly block out the sun and frighten small woodland creatures. A good grade of hair, no perm needed from appearances. And like me he loved baseball. He introduced himself, they spoke for a minute or two, and that was it before ya'll went off on your date.

That's all I knew about him for the first twenty years of my life, until me and you had *that* talk today. You know, the one where I built up the courage/idiocy to ask you for my father's name for the first time. And you went off on me to the *utmost*. Classic hissy fit with yelling, cursing. Foot stomping, speaking in tongues, and so on, and so forth.

But you finally spit it out. You confirmed it was the same as mine—just as Aunt Olivia had told me. I can't help but think maybe that's one reason why you can never quite treat me with fairness as your son, the way you embrace the other kids. Not because I am grown, or we battle, but because I have the name of a man that did you wrong. A man that was married when you met him in a bowling alley that you worked at part time while in school, when you were nineteen. A man that swore he'd leave his wife for you some day. A man that went to the same Catholic church as we did, as did his family—yet they nor he ever acknowledged us once before leaving, when I was around eight. Yeah, maybe that's why . . .

See, up until this point, that was all I cared to know. He's a stranger to me. I have no visions or delusions of a long-lost reunion. Simply put—if he didn't want me all these years, what could possibly change his mind now? But even if he did, I wouldn't want *him*. No, I don't long for a soapy reunion, with a prefabricated act of contrition on his part, or the typical explosive tirade on my part.

Conventional single mother wisdom says that, "A *sorry* daddy is better than *no* daddy." And I say they're right. But hold on, let me amend my previous statement. I do have something to say to the guy, a final send-off, which as seeing how we've never spoken before, would be an introductory send-off, I think.

Anyhow, Dad, I wish I were not such a disappointment, and could have been the beautiful boy most expect to see. But just know that I could never hate you, Father—much in the way that you could never love me.

Single moms will always rule.

- Manny

November 17, 1999

I probably should have gotten a minor in biochemistry. Or maybe alchemy. I've spent hundreds of hours researching chemical formulas, looking for a cure to a problem that has no kind of remedy whatsoever. I begged you several times to go to a NAMI support meeting, and you walked away from me each time, or say that you don't need it. At first, I was pretty mad, but after checking more into the group, my anger turned to disappointment. I read countless testimonials of people who say how it helped them get their life together.

Maybe I should just go by myself one day . . .

- Manny

February 29, 2000

Happy Leap Day. Is that a thing? Sorry it's been a while. I met Jesse Jackson this week when he did a march from Texas Southern to the University of Houston, for equal funding for HBCUs. I was actually able to break through the crowd (and his humongous body guards) to shake his hand. Takeaways? He is super tall. Like 6'2" or more maybe. Could never tell that from seeing him on TV. And he has very good hair. Like Billy Dee Williams good.

He told me (and the crowd at large I suppose), that "My mind is a pearl, and I can learn anything in this world."

I quietly thanked him. And one day, I just might believe him.

- Manny

April 7, 2000

In sociology class this week, we learned the nature of society's 'deviants.' Professor Curtis from that class is great. Shows up half the time, seems hung over, crazy stories that couldn't possibly be true, and told me he thought I was good writer and had an interesting voice/perspective. Very cool guy. Used to laugh and joke how he never showed up for class, and was probably super drunk. Then a TA came in today and told us he was extremely ill. And later rumors spread that he had in fact been a recovering alcoholic for decades. Going to say a prayer for him. He deserves that, and I deserve to feel bad . . .

Anyhow, unsurprisingly, many of the high-profile 'deviants' all had similar backgrounds. I'm speaking of characters as diverse as Lee Harvey Oswald to Ted Bundy having striking similarities in their upbringings. They each had domineering mothers, were schoolyard outcasts, and possessed self-loathing tendencies. So, all things considered, I suppose I could have turned out much, much worse . . . Which leads me to my thoughts on relationships, and how I am trying my best to avoid those self-hating, antisocial thoughts that others with some of my background traits have endured, that possibly lead them down a dark path. Let's talk about Alice, as an example.

I think her story best sums up what I'm trying to get to here. I met her in an English poetry class. She was not only cute with a great sense of humor, but played hoops for her high school team too—this was the Holy Grail for any B-boy of my generation. I got her number on our second day of class and we talked almost every night. I got her a really nice rosary for Easter, and she told me it was the 'sweetest thing ever.' Solid gold kid. And then I blew it. Put myself out there. On the last day of class, I showed up without my baseball cap, you know, to show her the *True* Manny. You know, what she could expect if we got any closer. How shall I put this—she bugged the hell out. I mean her eyes got as big as saucers when she saw my head and the scars. Her demeanor, body language, it all just completely closed off. And though she never point-blank said she was dropping me because I was ugly, I kind of wish she had. Instead, she never phoned again, never stopped by the student center where we used to hang out, etc. And then comes tonight, where D.J., and Jamon went to the movies, and guess who was there with her friends? Acted is if I did not exist. Wow. Quasimodo strikes out again.

As a result, I 'grew my hair down to there,' as the kids say. You know, because the braids would cover up my scars. Until it reached that point, I kept my hat on at all times. I'm not proud of my actions, but then again, I'm not really ashamed of them either. And if I need braids or a cap to have girls take me seriously, or put my best foot forward, then so be it. But of course, I'm lying. I *was* kind of ashamed. And embarrassed. And confused. Why couldn't people just accept me? Why didn't they know there was no difference between Manny with the braids, and Manny with the scars? I was just as funny, and smart and nice without a protective covering for my disfigurements. I could not for the life of me figure out how they could do it—disregard the feelings of a boy who might possibly be the greatest guy they've ever known (it's scientifically proven). But then again, that's precisely why they don't want me. Because I must be *too* nice and understanding—they figure I would have no choice but to be. Given my situation, I'd be grateful that any one of them would look at me twice, so I'd shower them with affection and smother them with emotion. And last time I checked, Cosmo wasn't writing any articles on "How to Snag the Needy and Desperate Guy of Your Dreams."

Well, that would not be the case at all. But no one will really give me the opportunity to prove it. I have therefore created an image of 'The Woman for Me.' However, I choose to focus on only the essentials this time. Like how she would be smart and compassionate. Comparable in height and humor. Have all-knowing eyes with the warmth of the sun (and of course rich, driving a Corvette, and a nice shape doesn't hurt either). One day I'll meet her, and she'll know me. She'll know the road I've traveled and the dreams I've accomplished. She'll know the failures I've learned from, and the mistakes I still regret. She'll know that although my family means everything to me, I'd have no trouble finding a place in my heart just for her.

Still Looking to Meet Virginia.

- Manny

November 6, 2000

I got jumped coming home from school tonight . . . I was riding the 44 bus and got off early. That was Mistake #1. I usually wait till it goes all the way around to Compaq (and grin and bear the evil looks of the Bus Driver Man, as they don't like people staying on during their layover), but this one time I decided to get off at the Exxon at the intersection of 1960 and 249.

I'm looking for traffic and watching both ways, etc., when I hear, "Hey Sand Nigger!" I didn't really catch it at first—not sure I heard what I thought I heard. Now, I've been around the block, and have been called the N-word *plenty* of times before, don't get me wrong. But it's usually murmured under someone's breath, done sneakily, and with a bit of hesitation. But this was flat out, no-holds barred racism, which was quite startling. So next, I instinctively turned to look for a Middle Eastern person (as this is whom the derogatory comment must have been directed toward, right?) to see if they were ok.

And then I heard, "Dune Coon, I know you hear me!" And that's when I realized that I, in fact, was the person that was not ok . . . This time the voice was closer, and I recognized that it had come from a white dude in a pickup truck (yeah, cliché city, right?). I'm pretty sure I saw him and his two or three friends as I walked by Exxon give a mean stare. But I've been getting those for over two decades, so it didn't bother me much as I made my way around the road's loop.

The streets were dead quiet. First thing I did was look to see who else was out here to help me, and possibly scare them off. No one. Then I remembered that I did not pay my cell phone bill and it was cut off—damn you Cingular—so no cops. Then I seriously thought about beginning to run. And then I *did* run.

One hopped out, and then the others drove around and cut me off. Bam. Fully unopened beer can against my head from 25 feet away maybe (racist or not, that was pretty good throw). Then one catches up with me. I drop the book bag and go for what I know. Which isn't much. It's not like I'm big like D.J. or Jamon and have been brawling all my life. Nope, I did what came instinctively—tried to wrestle him down. Worked for a bit, until his friend came and kicked me in the back. And then the multitude of blows followed. And then came more cursing. Another beer can or two, and then some spitting.

They left after about five minutes, saying on the way out I should, "Get a job' and go back home." I started to say, "Dude, I'm black and was born here." But I ultimately decided against it, seeing as how they might decide they needed to kick my ass for an entirely *different* hateful reason.

My ribs hurt pretty bad, got a black eye, and they carved out some new terrain in my back with their boots, but I'm still fit to fly. I'll go to the Acres Homes Clinic tomorrow and have somebody give me the once over. The school doctor costs too much. Wish they didn't wail on me so good that I couldn't catch the license plate . . .

I must admit it's pretty funny. Moved the kids out of the ghetto, all the way out to the nice suburbs of Northwest Houston in 1960 to be safe, and this is where I catch a hate crime? For the wrong reason at that. Guess I need to shave this beard I've been growing for way too long, start wearing my pants saggy again, so people realize who they are dealing with. Or at least think I might be able to fight back . . .

Thanksgiving is in two or three weeks. I guess for the giving season they decided to give me a beatdown . . .

- Manny

December 15, 2000

School is winding down, and I might be graduating in January (a semester early)—knock on wood. In Health class I finally decided to ask this girl who's been nice to me—Joy—for her number. She's like twenty-six or twenty-seven, and works as a dietician for the City Health Department. No kids, and no man in the picture. I can then only logically assume she did a lengthy prison bid and that's why she's so late wrapping up her bachelors . . .

When I *finally* build up the nerve to ask her out today before class is over, what was her response? "Why?" I start stuttering and stammering, "Umm, I umm, thought maybe umm, you and me . . . I mean, I and you, could umm . . ."

She bursts out laughing and apologizes. Says she never gets asked for her number much, dudes think she's mean and stand-offish (*the hell* you say?). But she gives it to me, and it has seven digits, so I'm hopeful that it's real, and says she'd like to do something sometime.

She is cute as cute can be. Really smart, pleasant, and fun too. She liked a paper I read her that I wrote on Chris Cornell and his *Euphoria Morning* album, and said she thought I could do that for a living. I don't know if I actually have the nerve to call her. She's older, *way* out of my league . . . I gotta meditate on this one . . .

Time to go looking for Christmas stuff. I'm going to go get the kids cable TV this year (they've been *dying* for it). And you, maybe the good old Estee Lauder perfume you adore. See, you think I don't notice that stuff just because we fight. And argue. And fight. And bicker . . . But I see the good as well as the bad, Selita. I see it all.

- Manny

May 11, 2001

I graduated from college today. It was a long and winding road, but I made it.

What the future may hold is anyone's guess . . .

- Manny

June 22, 2001

You birthday was yesterday . . . The Discovery Channel had on a great investigative report on schizophrenia. They showed some really detailed and great success stories and the drug/therapy combos that got the people there. And more importantly—they talked about the drugs that either did not work or had bad side effects associated with them. Super helpful.

There were a lot of good case studies presented. Like the NASA engineer with depression and bipolar disorder who took lithium and got her job back. Or the lady who considered her daily dose of 360 mg of Effexor to be the only reason she could function in a world she feared had long since left her by. And then there's the schizophrenic woman taking a combo of Zyprexa and Paxil, which gave her family true hope that she will never slip away again.

There were others—many others—who found some semblance of success through medication, psychotherapy, or some combination thereof. And I won't even lie—I know I'm a terrible guy—because instead of wishing these survivors well, my only thought is, when will we get our happy ending?

I've looked into every medication known to man, watched every documentary I could get my hands on. I've read every investigative report, lifted numerous medical journals from doctor's offices. One report on the A&E cable channel stood out. A group called the Stanley Foundation worked with patients suffering from schizophrenia. They told viewers to not believe in doctors who say therapy is all you need. They said that method was successful in only 5 percent of studies. A combination of medication and therapy is seen as the only viable route. I often find myself asking what could possibly work for you. The Vega Nerve Stimulator being tested at Baylor University, where an implant device similar to a pacemaker is inserted and sends impulses to the brain every five minutes to battle depression? Or a mix of drug therapy to battle each element of your psychosis? However, this leads to questions of side effects, or the drugs battling each other. I've read plenty of stories along these lines as well.

I choose to follow the advice of a man who works in the Fountain House program, Dr. Aguilla, I believe. His method is to give tough love to schizophrenics in order to help them reclaim their lives. It suits me. No, it suits us. Whenever you slip off, I zap you back to reality. You refuse to buy dish soap at the store; I assure you no one's after you there. You won't use the milk I buy; I drink it first in front of you to prove it's actually not poison. What can I say? If it works, it works. Plato's nowhere in my league. I taped it and wrote everything down and will try to do a little research on my end.

There was also Dr. Atchison who advised me to get you into therapy first, to appeal to your ego if need be. What might this involve? Well, to be frank, lying my butt off.

So yesterday, I gave it a try. Saying that I did not want you to get help for me, or for the sake of the kids. That it would be all for *you*, Selita. That you're relatively young (forty-three now), and that if you took steps to get your sickness under control, you could get back in the workforce, and finish your master's perhaps. Maybe meet a good guy, and so forth. But only, *only* if you got help first. And I went on as to how I knew you could not possibly be happy, and being such a smart lady, you must know there is a better life for you out there within your reach. Hell, you lived it for about twenty-five years; if you wanted it back, then damn it, all you had to do was reach out your hand to me! This train evidently ain't coming on its own, so why not nudge it along with a little counseling here, a little drug therapy there. Talk to a doctor (not necessarily mine) about the hard life you've had, and how it may have affected a decision or two of yours along the way.

The bottom line—do it for *yourself* Selita. Get better for you, while there's still time to do so. And even though there's been so much between us, you have to believe me when I say that you'll feel so much better if you build up the courage to help yourself, as opposed to me *forcing* you into it. Oh yeah, that was my 'A' material right there. I put it all on the line. I talked *to you* instead of *at you*. There was no cursing, no yelling, no reindeer games of any type. Just a boy talking to his mother, telling the truth, straight from his heart.

Man, I wove that speech together so intricately and earnestly that it actually reminded me how I felt about you early on in our life together. But just like every time before—and since this little grandstand—you turned me down. However, this time, your reply was priceless: "God bless your kind heart, Manny Williams. But don't bother with something that is none of your concern." Hallmark never said it better.

- Manny

September 11, 2001

Not many words. Just tears and fear. When you woke me up to tell me what was happening, I thought you were having an episode. And then when I saw it on the news, it looked like something out of an Arnold Schwarzenegger movie. I thought it was fake.

God bless everyone lost, and I will say a prayer for them and their families.

- Manny

September 25, 2001

I got a call from an old girlfriend yesterday Shawana, to be more precise. I gave her a ring, or she called me, I forget which out of the blue. We hadn't seen each other in about four years. I called it off back in the day over nonsense, to be more precise. We decided to catch up and, planned on meeting up at Willowbrook Mall. Before I got there, I had to drop off our car insurance payment because it was over a month late. Backing out of the lot, I hit a parked car, and left a small to medium-ish scratch on the bumper. I left a note with all of my information. It's the right thing to do after all.

Me and Miss Puppy Love met up and it was like nothing had changed. Until the moment she decided to tell me she had met someone at Prairie View University. And that she liked him. And that we were way over, it was a short-term high school thing, and could only be friends, at best. Damn. Now she could have told me all of this over the phone. I mean, *double damn*. Worst of all, I gave her a handmade doll that Rosalind had created for me as a present. She does great work, and you couldn't tell it apart from an antique store-bought doll. I was in an evil place after that meeting. I didn't yell or curse at her, but I was dying inside. I broke all kinds of land speed records on the ride back home. I took the exact same route and passed the car insurance building. Out of straight curiosity I checked, and lo and behold, the car I hit was still in the same spot. What about the note, you might ask? It was in the same spot under the windshield wiper. Right until I took it off and ripped it up. Why should I be the only one to have a bad day, I figured. Yeah, not my brightest moment by any means. But I couldn't go through with it. Once I got in the car, I couldn't help but think that maybe this car was owned by a single mother. And if she was working this late (past 7 p.m.), then she must need all her money, and if she had to pay to repair this then she'd have to work more shifts which would keep her away from her kids and . . . you get the idea.

Guilt—the greatest gift of all.

- Manny

November 6, 2001

The Buffy musical episode was tonight—and it was awesome. The prophecies were true. Spike's song was literally, the Best . . . Well, maybe it was a tie with the Xander and Anya duet. That was really funny. I just found out that Spike is like forty in real life. I thought he was like twenty-five to thirty—same range as the other young actors. He's evidently on that Brad Pitt fountain of youth serum they keep loosely guarded from the rest of us beasts.

- Manny

November 29, 2001

Aunt Erma passed today . . .I was at the hospital at the very beginning when she had her stroke. I would sit with her while I studied my law school exam book. She mostly slept, but when she was awake, she recognized me.

I took Mama Dear to see her a few times, too. And as the weeks went on, instead of every day, I started going once a week. Then once every other week. Down to none at all. I just could not bear to see her look like that. But that's no excuse. I should have sucked it up. I heard she was really bad, but Little Greg said she asked about me. I never heard that until now . . . God, I'm pathetic. Can't find courage for an old lady on her deathbed, without whom I never would have gotten into college. I feel great about myself. But there

I go being selfish— because this day is in no way about me. I'm going to go drive over to Mama Dear's house and take the kids to cheer her up.

- Manny

December 8, 2001

I'm still having a hard time finding work. It's so bad, I'm up at Compaq assembling computers. Graveyard shift, ten-hour days, four nights a week. I've been here a week and already hate it. At least I stuck it out at Target for three months before quitting . . .

I have a bachelor's degree in Poli Sci, and am working part time in a warehouse, which is not a dishonorable position, but it's not the career for me. I guess on a very small scale this is somewhat how foreign residents feel when they are doctors and engineers in their home countries but get to America where their degrees are not recognized and find themselves working is restaurants and taxis. Yeah, good old political science. For what that degree has turned out to be worth, I might as well have gotten one in Eastern Mysticism or something.

I'm trying, Selita. I know you don't believe it based on the fact that you put a note on my door saying I am not, what was it, "pulling my fair share" around the house. No notes needed. You've told me so often throughout my life about how worthless and what a disappointment I am that it just plays on a loop in my brain at this point.

- Manny

April 3, 2002

Some people say that me continuing to try and help you even though you do all that you can to make this an impossible task is evidence of me having a hero complex. Whereas I would argue that my hero complex comes as a direct result of me watching too much *Superman* as a child.

A few days ago, I ran into an old high school classmate who asked me what I had been up to lately. My reply was, "The same stuff I'm always doing—looking forward to dying alone." Now I just said that for the shock value/a cry for help, but she took it as a joke. Close enough. But I have always felt that it would be my inevitable fate, so there was more than a kernel of truth in that line . . .

Whenever I'm asked if I want to have children someday, I always say I can't have kids. Not because of a medical condition or anything, but because I simply can't afford them. Having so many sisters and a brother, I have needed twice what I earn just to look after them. So that is an entirely acceptable and appropriate response, I feel. But an entirely honest assessment of the question would be that I feel I have no right bringing a child into a world that I have come nowhere near close to adjusting to myself. Now with my siblings, I can help them guilt-free due to the fact that they are already here and are not of my making—if that makes any sense at all. I didn't bring them into this broken world, so any assistance I can give them is basically bonus points for them. Misguided or not, there lot in life is so bad, that I pretty much can't do any more harm to them by pitching in.

People often gripe about terrible dads. Some on how their dads leaving them at the age of three, or verbally abusing them, and so on. Well, unless they were true monsters, I would have been fine with any one of those fathers. As you are well aware, I have never even seen my dad. That's how much he thought of me. What could the reason possibly be? For him wanting nothing to do with me, that is. Was it because I was unplanned or that he wanted to avoid child support payments? Or maybe that he simply didn't want anything to do with you? Or because he was already married, as I heard? Maybe. Do I think you have held these factors against me my entire life in one way or another? Definitely. Do I hold this against you? Not anymore.

We have had some laughs over the years, but there were so many bad times, that the good fade from memory. Like when I asked you to help me with my math homework and you told me you had no choice but to go purse shopping. Or, when I asked you why you dated so many guys and you said it was because 'I want to get you a stepdad.' I replied that I felt I would prefer to have a *mother* . . . And then your final reply was slapping the taste out of my mouth. There was you breaking into my monkey-themed piggy bank in order to buy drugs for Arthur Lee. And finally, I remember you showering gifts in an attempt to impress your friends, coworkers, and basically everyone under the sun—except your son.

I will also admit that I certainly still hold a grudge over my accident, and the subsequent settlement that you bungled. Twenty-four thousand. That's how much my face, your child's face, was worth to them. You, too, I suppose, since you had to sign off on it. I guess I could have walked away with nothing, but when people get a million dollars for getting coffee burns on their laps at a fast-food restaurant, it just kind of puts me in a New York state of mind. Mama Dear says she tried to talk you into waiting for a high-profile attorney to be available to try the case, but you had to do it your way. You wouldn't wait until the attorney could return from an oil rig accident case and you decided to press ahead with the suit. Now whenever anyone finds out about my accident, they naturally assume I made out like a bandit and am thus set for life. I don't bother getting into the shape of things, so I nod and smile, telling them, "Yeah. God has really been good to me."

I really need you to understand why I behave the way I do toward you sometimes. I'm speaking of the days I yell, or the weeks where I walk past you countless times but have nothing to say. It's just that I have not let go of after all these years. As they say, a child *never* forgets. And as difficult at times as it is for me to admit, I am still your child.

- Manny

August 17, 2002

Well, I'm finally about to start South Texas College of Law. I deferred admission last year, so now it's time to either get down to business— or get off the pot. As you know by now, I have moved out of the apartment. But don't fret, I'm in the complex right next door to y'all. I'll be staying with Jamon in Copper Creek Apartments. He really needs the help. I'm going to try to get him enrolled in North Harris Community College—I'll even take the tests and fill out the paperwork if I have to. I've just got to get him off the streets. He's seventeen and living like a fifty-year-old convict . . .

- Manny

September 12, 2002

So, I dropped out of law school. Yeah, that was quick right? I just wasn't feeling it. I'd been out of school and working too long to sit there and take notes and do homework again. Plus, y'all kept on calling me to come over and help with this and that while I tried to study. Plus, Jamon had girls, and friends, and enemies in and out of the house at all hours of the nights. And . . . I wonder, when will I find my piece of mind?

Okay, I feel much better now that I've gotten that out. I'm in good standing because I left before any grades came out. Given that, I could always go back in a semester. Or in a year.

- Manny

December 15, 2002

I have an interview for a good job, finally. It is in the car insurance field. I had my best suit on, and Dominque helped with my tie. You even gave me the rare compliment: "Ooh, Mr. Manny Williams sure is looking nice today. He could probably go out there and get him a white woman." Me and Dominque laughed for like thirty-seven minutes straight.

On a deadly serious note, I ran to the music store to get the new Nas album, *God's Son*, and it's the *real deal*. There's *I Can* inspiring black children all over the world, letting them know they descend from Kings and Queens, and have greatness in their blood. But *the* song is *Thugz Mansion*. It's a duet with Pac, talking of a heavenly mansion where poor people get to go to after they pass, and it's heartbreaking, and so good. He gives his own mother Ann Jones, as well as Afeni Shakur, Tupac's mom, maybe the greatest shout-outs that perhaps any mothers have received since, well, *Dear Mama*. I have listened to it about a million times, and am not gonna stop anytime soon.

Nas is a true poet. So talented at such an early age, his verses are cinematic. I am super glad that he made his comeback last year when he put out *Ether* and *One Mic*. He has something to say, and the tools to say it convincingly. Talent *always* wins out.

- Manny

January 3, 2003

Stephanie got a ticket today for being out past curfew at the movies. I didn't even know Houston had a curfew? It's going to cost me like $300 to pay for this, I bet. Just what I needed. I start my new job at Progressive Insurance in a little while. I'll be doing auto claims. You know, like in the commercials where the guy comes up to the scene of the accident in the little Progressive SUV? Well, that will be me. Or shall I say, it will be me in about two months, once training is done. I'm going to beg Janet to borrow some money to pay this ticket. Talk to you in a couple of days probably.

- Manny

January 6, 2003

There was a notice to vacate on your apartment door when I came by today. Why Selita? I *gave* you the money for the rent—what did you do with it?! Out buying shoes? Or that junk from the Home

Shopping Network? Giving it to one of your 'boyfriends' again so you can pay his bills while your kids are about to be put on the street! You are so lucky and you don't even know it. I wish I had somebody to cover my back and erase my mistakes all the time. It must really be nice.

That lady in the apartment office said it's just a form letter, so if I pay today it'll be okay . . . This is getting so old, and I will take action to change things soon. That, I *promise*.

- Manny

January 20, 2003

I started with Progressive today, and I'm still working part time at Gallup too. I got Jamon a job up there, but he quit/got fired, naturally. Then, he was working security and called me up one night to say he, "was just *too high* to go to work." Lovely. He had me call his boss and pretend like he was in jail and that was the reason he couldn't make his shift.

I also re-enrolled him at South Texas College of Law for this spring. I'll work at Progressive during the day, take part-time night classes during the week for law school, and work at Gallup on Friday, Saturday, and Sunday. Wow. That's stressful just typing it up.

Well, I have to run and get some boots that are made for walking— because I have a feeling I'm about to be doing quite a bit of that for the next long while.

Wish me well.

- Manny

February 19, 2003

Well, I dropped out of law school. *Again* . . .It was just too much to take. I was way behind in the readings and I had to work the night of the orientation, so the professors were like, "Who the hell are you?" when I showed up.

I actually saw someone in class there that I knew, Jennifer. In case you don't remember, it's *The Jennifer* from the Kermit The Frog story when I was an undergrad. What are the chances? Anyway, her hair is no longer platinum blonde now. It's her natural brunette. But I wouldn't forget those green bug eyes anywhere. When I caught her attention in the classroom at law school, she just stared right through me. Maybe she just didn't notice me with my braids and the thirty extra pounds I've packed on since my undergrad years. Or maybe she did—and just didn't care. Another one of the world's great mysteries, I suppose.

- Manny

March 15, 2003

I'm in the Sunshine State of Arizona. No wait . . . that's Florida, right? Well, I'm in whatever state Phoenix is in. Progressive is sending all of the trainees to get their auto certification for casualty insurance for a two and a half week training. I have met some really friendly people during my time training, like Tri a.k.a. Joe (who helped me push my car when it broke down in the parking garage), Eddie, Chad (who went to Stephen F. Austin and looks like a future politician), Jenny, and one guy who looked just like a twenty-five-year-old Mr. Burns and drinks Seabreeze's. I fell on my first ski slope while under their employ, too (the teacher told me some junk about making my legs look like French fries and pizza—whatever). I know what you are thinking, how did we ski in the desert? Well, if you drive two hours north from Phoenix, you hit Flagstaff which has mountains, much higher elevations, and snow. The temperature dropped about 5 degrees every 15 minutes we drive. I had never seen anything like it before. And the winding mountain roads are right out of NASCAR. One guy fell asleep on the way back to the hotel and we all screamed, just knowing we were going to fly off the side of the mountain. Good times. There was a Native American casino up there as well, with a strange mix of characters, from rich preppies to working class indigenous people, to wide-eyed tourists like us, to guys standing outside doing security holding shotguns and wearing gang colors. I really had lots of fun, but in the end, once again, I just did feel as if I belong. And once back from the ski trip, I received a missed call from the kids saying you started acting up again as well, and just like that, the party was over, and Cinderalla's glass slipper fell off.

Right before the trip I broke up with this girl named Jamie who I've been seeing for the last few months. She's really nice. A Jehovah's Witness actually, so that made her pretty sheltered and shy—right about my speed. She actually used to date the brother (Ramone) of the twins (Rodney and Ronald) from my middle and high school. Their mom really has a thing with the letter 'R' I guess . . . He works in Loss Prevention at Target I think, and is a little wilder and more street smart than them. She was working in the Sears shoe department in Willowbrook Mall when I went to get my shoes for the big Progressive interview. I smiled the whole way through, and when she asked if there was anything else I needed, I replied, "Yes, your phone number, please." Yeah, I know, too smooth for words, right?

I guess all those years hanging with Jamon finally paid off, because it worked.

I think in the end we were a little too alike. Get two shy people together and they can literally sit all day and not say/do anything. A nice girl indeed—just not the one for me. Okay, got to go pack now. Ciao.

- Manny

P.S. I'll send y'all a postcard and some extra money—they are actually paying us twice; we get our normal salary *plus* expense money per day.

March 23, 2003

I finally caught the Dave Chapelle show tonight, which I heard about, but had never seen. I am in Austin (rode up on a weekend trip with Greg and Rosalind) to help Lynell move into her new house in Pflugerville. It's a small nice little suburb outside of Austin. *Really* nice home. Played basketball with her husband Eugene, hung out with my Lynell's boys Matt and Chris a bit, then Little Greg came over, and it's always great to see him.

We got some chicken after we finished moving, and saw the show. The whole episode was super funny, but he did an impression of R. Kelly that had us *howling*. Literally crying because it was so funny. It was beyond risqué, kind of in poor taste, but man . . . it was like nothing we had ever seen before. I would not be shocked if R. Kelly tried to sue him, fight him, kill him after seeing that. It was that insane.

- Manny

April 14, 2003

I quit Progressive today. I am actually not home but in a hotel lobby in San Diego. Jamon and I packed up at one in the morning, caught a cab to the bus station, and then the first Greyhound bus heading west—and just never got off till the final destination. We stopped by San Antonio, El Paso, Phoenix (again for me), I think New Mexico, and finally arrived after like two days of travel. Of course, we promptly fell out, so he has his hotel in the hood section of downtown so he can be near his 'people,' while I am staying in a nice spot near the convention centers.

I let him keep the rental car. Too many hills down here for me—and the highway is *crazy*. It's like when you go to The Woodlands and you have to drive *up* in order to get *off* the freeway, instead of just being able to take an exit road down below. Confused the hell out of me. We almost ended up in Anaheim my first time behind the wheel . . . I met a girl down here—Danielle. She is super cute and in school. Trains as a dancer (Modern, jazz, tap? No idea), I think, in her spare time when she isn't a waitress and goes to school.

I told Progressive that I had to take a leave because you were ill, which is *technically* true, except I said it was your heart as opposed to your head. Minor detail . . . I merely walked out at lunch one day, and never returned. I guess you wanna ask what I'm running from, huh, Selita? In all honesty, I think I'm running from *everything*. You being sick, the kids needing me, commitment, maturity, responsibility, a life I did not see myself leading . . .

I think I'm ready to finally make my great escape. I've been plotting this for a while. Saved the money I earned during training, plus my income tax. I have like $8,000 total. I applied for a similar insurance position with Geico and have an interview for their Poway (close to San Diego) location set up. They actually offered me a job in Tucson in a new operation they just started, but I passed. If it was Phoenix, then no doubt . . . But Tucson? No thanks. I'll try and keep in touch as best I can.

- Manny

May 2, 2003

I am officially back home from San Diego now. Things cost *a lot* more than I thought. I found a temp gig—Jamon found nothing. We fought the *entire* time of the trip. Mama Dear kept calling and asking when I would be back. Evidently, a neighbor saw me and Jamon packing up at one in the morning with big duffel bags, and when Brit went by our house, she talked to her about it. Guess she thought it might have been a body in there or something . . . Looks like California Dreamin' is literally just that, a dream and nothing more.

- Manny

June 21, 2003

Got a great birthday present for you, Selita—I'm moving back in! Yeah, just what you always wanted, but were afraid to ask for, right? I'll be on the floor in the front with Dante, but I plan to use the money I refrained spending on the trip to get us a three-bed apartment again.

Wow, just three months ago I had two jobs, an apartment, a girl-friend, and a decent car. Oh yeah, lest I forget, Jamon *totaled* my Lumina last week. I woke up to go the corner store for soda and chips, and went outside to find the front seat resting comfortably in the backseat. He was in the house sleeping—with five of his closest friends. I kicked everybody out and me and him had a knockdown, drag-out fight inside and outside, up and down the stairs.

I love him like a brother . . . but all he does is *use* me.

- Manny

❧

June 14, 2003

Saw the Red Hot Chili Peppers at The Woodlands today. Man, I love them. Ever since John Frusciante came back, they have been going so hard. Dave Navarro is super cool, but Frusciante is the missing ingredient. Their latest album is so beautiful—and *funky*. Love *The Zephyr Song*, *Universally Speaking*, *Can't Stop*, and please, please do not let me forget *Warm Tape*.

I was going to go see them with Jamon and his super pretty cousin Tracy (on Beverly's side—no blood relation to me). I had three tickets, but then I realized I hated him for wrecking my car. So, I gave the tickets to my friend Roger from Gallup for him and his girl, and I flew solo.

A day this beautiful almost makes me forget how bad you've been making me feel since I moved back in. *Almost.* I'm your son, Selita, and you talk to me like I'm some kind of *animal*. You always refer to me 'encroaching' on 'you and your children.' What the hell am I, if not your child? I was there before any of them were born, or even thought of . . . All's well, though . . . for tonight, at least.

- Manny

June 30, 2003

It just got to be too much . . . I did not want to have to commit you again, Selita, but I promise you gave me *no choice*. I for sure did not want the kids to see you get led away by those Sheriff deputies, but you won't take your medicine. I'm starting to think with all your threats against me, you may even turn violent. Your birthday was not even two weeks ago. I got cake and ice-cream, and for the briefest of seconds, we seemed like more than the bottom-dwelling, gone-to-hell brood we act like all the time.

I'm not surprised you didn't speak when I came to visit today at MHMR. I suppose it's hard to be Ms. Manners when you're sent away on an involuntarily hold kicking and screaming to a mental hospital . . . No pushback at all from the family, to my face that is. What they are whispering behind my back I'll never know. I just hope you let these people help you this time. Please agree to take your medicine and get better, because your kids need to see you that way. *All* your children, Selita.

I'm sorry.

- Manny

July 1, 2003

So, I've been going through your things, I won't even deny it. I want to see where all the money you've been given has been going. I found something that says you've been getting an increased SSI benefits since

Ray died as well? An extra $700 a month you never mentioned all the times you were hounding me to pay your bills, while I'm pawning *every-thing* I own to get groceries for the kids and keep the lights and water on? Lovely as ever. I see you are still paying for your ex-con boyfriend Robert's phone and gas bill? That stops today, thank you very much. Service disconnected.

I'm marching up to the Social Security office the first minute I can to report you for mismanagement. Sick or not, this is ridiculous. I may even go for custody. At this point, any and everything is on the table. The rage I have inside *knows no limits.*

I bought you a car, got y'all several apartments in increasingly nice neighborhoods. Paid all the bills, kids school expenses, and even paid off your crooked lawyer, who knew that Rays ex-wife had already received his pension and life insurance benefits before taking your case. I have liter-ally used every penny to my name and then some to support you and the kids. All my settlement money from Hermann—$24k—out the door. My refund money from my scholarships and grants, plus all the jobs I've worked over the years—gone. Five credit cards—maxed out. Meanwhile, you deprive your children, spend money on random me, hide money, lie, and treat me like an ATM . . . and a fool.

Good thing you're in that hospital right now, because I might be in jail with the thoughts I'm having.

- Manny

July 3, 2003

Oh my God, They let you out of the hospital and didn't even call first. When they said they were keeping you past the 72 hour hold for the first time, and that you had actually agreed to take some medication, I should have known it was too good to be true. That you had come to your senses, were putting your health and your family first, and had decided to focus on your health. Believing that should have earned me a trip inside for being the true crazy person. Turns out they mixed your release info with another patient, and you were out the door with no expended treatment the first chance you got, per usual . . . Did you see me at the post office? When Jamon and I pulled up and I saw you outside the door, I damn near had a heart attack. I can just imagine the mood you'll be in when you get back to the house. Guess it's time for my chickens to come home to roost . . .

- Manny

August 19, 2003

I'm back at The University of Houston. I will take some classes as a post-bac in Biology. I'm thinking maybe I can return to my science roots and make a last pie-in-the-sky run at medical school before I get way over the hill. Even better news, though, is that I got us approved for a much nicer apartment. It's more like a condo. No gimmicks or anything . . . got the keys in my hand. It's a three bedroom with a study that can be converted. It has a huge garage and even huger backyard—wonder who's going to cut that? Dante better eat his Wheaties, that's all I'm saying.

I have my own apartment, I am getting steady temp work, and have the grant refund checks for the difference between my stipend and the actual school cost (borrowing and sharing textbooks instead of buying to save even more). I have a strange feeling that this might work. For once, whatever this is that we have, might actually work . . .

- Manny

November 28, 2003

Mama Dear strikes again . . . I dropped my classes, and I'm breaking my lease to get out of my apartment. Jamon's saying don't do it because I'll never get another shot like this to break away, but Mama Dear just kept playing on my emotions, saying how much y'all missed and needed me. Saying that the kids were doing so bad in school without my help . . . Same old story.

I am twenty-four years old. I need to move on with my life. *Please.* I'm tired of being a beauty school dropout. It's like that Elvis song, "I'm caught in a trap. I can't walk out." All because I love y'all too much. But one day—when I have the nerve—I'll get ghost. I'll call and send money, but it'll be from afar.

So, let it be written, so let it be done (Pharaoh style).

- Manny

January 23, 2004

I started a second job last week. It's with a phone survey company— somewhat like Gallup—called Voter Consumer Research. I know, bottom feeding, but it's keeping y'all laced in cable and jiffy pop pop-corn, so it can't be that bad.

I met a few alright folks up there. One guy named Brent who's like thirty-six, I think. He takes care of his mom, too, except unlike you she's rich, and sane. Just kidding there, no hard feelings, okay. There's also a cute girl named Stephanie. She's, nineteen years old, and from Vermont. Brent really likes her. We sit up and throw paper balls at her while she's on the phone. She gets flustered and we laugh and laugh. Could be a fun distraction.

- Manny

February 18, 2004

When I made it to work today, I saw this huge white guy was at the front door just waiting. He had hardcore tattoos, and looked shady as can be. Like super skeevy, as in he had a traumatic *After School Special* written about him and his crimes in the past. Definitely filled with bad intentions, and the means to make them happen. I got in and called Brent. I wanted him to be careful. From her description, I think it could be Stephanie's ex. He followed her from Vermont and has a restraining order against him up there. Brent called our manager Pete, who notified security. They inter-cepted the dude and called the cops. Turns out it was him—and he had a huge butterfly knife in his jacket. Pete, Brent, Stephanie, and a few others are calling me a hero because there's no telling what might have gone down if they walked by that door together hand in hand and old buddy saw them. I shrugged it off—yet secretly, I glow on the inside due to the praise. Everybody congratulates me except Kelly, a girl up there I like. She could not be any more indifferent.

Oh well, those are the breaks.

- Manny

March 22, 2004

I quit my temp gig and started working at United Recovery Systems. It's a credit card collection agency that's a long drive to work on Harwin (Southwest side), but the pay is good. Met some funny guys named Winston, Herman, and Marcus. They consider themselves to be the last three players on the planet, so they crack me up.

I think I'm going to shave my head for good today. Mama Dear in no way understands why I would do so—especially after all of the pain and agony from my numerous surgeries. I just go in cycles. Grow it for six months, then cut it off. Grow it for two years, and then chop it off. But the truth is, it's starting to thin out now. Not from baldness, but me pulling it out due to that nervous condition. She always told me this would happen, and I'll be damned if it didn't finally come to pass. Thanks for always being right, Granny.

I couldn't help myself, though. The only thing I loved more than tossing my braids around like a 'little white girl' was to tease and pull my hair to the brink of ruin. Same thing with my eyelashes. When something is on my mind, I'll sit there and play with them for hours on end, pulling out multiple strands without even realizing it.

I'm too old for braids anyway. At least, that's what I'll repeat over and over as I cry myself to sleep the next few months.

- Manny

June 15, 2004

Dante overflowed the toilet again. What is his *problem*? He puts an ungodly amount of paper in there each time. I told him he only needs a small amount to get the job done, but, it is what it is . . .

When we won the court case after Ray died and got the kids back, we were so excited. But then we wondered, now what do we do with them? Where would they sleep? How would they eat? You were still out of sorts and not working, to boot. The other side of the kids' family had already accessed Ray's pension and life insurance policies. We heard it was divided between Tam and Ray, who should not be denied seeing as how they were Ray's kids. But they were not his *only* kids.

The kids would have to cram into Mama Dear's with the rest of us. I would be graduating in a few months, so that would open a little room. Nah, scratch that. It turned out that Mama Dear had other things lined up for me. She said getting the kids back was only the initial battle, and that raising them would comprise the war. My response was, "Good luck with that. I'm off to college."

I have mentioned numerous times that Mama Dear suggested I might want to stay close to home—the University of Houston per-haps—so that I could keep an eye on you and the kids. I, on the other hand, suggested that she keep all further suggestions to herself. I then told her flat out that there was no way I would consider that. I mean, I had put in my time on Mulberry Drive, I did my part, played my role. I followed the rules—no going out, no drinking or smoking. Worked every year since I was thirteen. I testified, stood by you even when you refused to acknowledge me. Handed over half of my paycheck to you each week without so much as a thank you. Well, that was it. There was no way I was sticking around for more. I needed to leave. I *deserved* to leave. And there was nothing she could do to change my mind.

But grandmother's, of course, have a special power all unto their own. Her pimp hand is way stronger than Snoop and Ice-T's *combined*. And eventually, you got your children back, but what did they get? To be crammed into a sixty-year-old house with eight other relatives. Sharing beds, using one bathroom, just enough food to avoid hunger pains. And last, but certainly not least, an older brother who didn't know which end was up, and a mentally ill mother who loved them with all her misguided heart.

The best way I can explain it, Selita, is to say that it was straight up *Jurassic Park*. How they basically spent too much time with, "Whether they could, they didn't stop to think if they should." I kind of think that's what we did in our rush to reunite you with the kids. But it is what it is, or it was what it was—you be the judge.

Regardless, we did get the kids back, and I made up my mind to stay and help out. The reason, well, had something to do with the fact that they needed me, and, I suppose I needed them in turn. Not because it would make my life more fulfilling, but because I was unsure what I would do with myself, or to myself, if I turned my back on them. General uncertainty also played a huge factor in my decision. I was not sure how they would be treated by anyone else. How much love would they receive, and what sacrifices would be made on their behalf? Would they be looked at as individuals over there, or merely lumped together? Would they be looked down upon as their mother had been? Would they remain together or be split up amongst aunts and uncles? Who would be the one to stay up late at night searching for ways to make their lives better? Who would scheme and dream about taking them out of the hood and into a better place? Who else could possibly want all of this and more for them—than me?

I decided to play the odds. And, as you were quick to point out to me on more than one occasion, it didn't require bravery or courage at all. As the old saying goes, "Courage is nothing more than being scared of something, and doing it anyway." In the history of time, other people have taken on more, with a lot less help. As for whether it will work out in the long term, well, the jury's still out on that one.

Waiting patiently as ever for the jury's decision . . .

- Manny

October 22, 2004

So here are your kids, listed in the reverse order of who I love most Just Kidding. *Mostly.* Stephanie. "Mother, mother, Manny wants a brother." D.J. and Olivia sung this to you in 1986 and I busted out laughing, mainly because it was true. But along came Steph, who in one swift moment ended my reign as the overlord-style only child. Before her appearance, I never had to share or split my time—not with Mama Dear, that is. Now, at first, I was curious to see what all the fuss was about babies. I held her a few times, and by then I was good. They could take her right back from whence she came from for all I cared. For one, she cried *so much* as a child. She always seemed to keep either an ear infection, colic, or a fever. I also thought it was pretty freaky how she seemed to change colors all of a sudden. She was a light brown color when she was first born, but after a few months she got to be pretty dark. I eventually picked up on the fact that with black babies their initial color isn't always how they are going to look. The color of the tip of their ears is more indicative of how they'll turn out in the end. Pretty wild.

Me and Steph have waged some *tremendous* battles over the years—from the mundane issue of who got the last cup of chocolate milk (easy—always me), up to the larger one of me attempting to parent her. She was quick to tell me "I was not her daddy" when I corrected her, and I accepted that from her for a long time. But when she was about twelve years old and I was nineteen, I snapped back, "You're right, because your dad was a crack head that used to whoop on Selita." Now it shut her up as planned, and she huffed and puffed while storming off, but I felt pretty bad afterwards. I never said anything of that nature to her again—I had no right. It's not as if my dad was some beacon of virtue by comparison . . .

In all honesty, I didn't really care for Stephanie for the longest time; she absolutely felt (feels?) the same way about me. She wouldn't bow down to me, and I'm man enough to say that truly worked my nerves. This went on till she was about seventeen. I figured out early on that she wouldn't comply with my rules because she had grown up with me. I was only seven when she was born; she had even seen me in my Superman pajamas for goodness sake. Kind of her to demand she respect my authority when that's on the table . . . Whereas the other kids and I have a larger age gap between us, Steph views me as more of a peer, than a *leader*. And so that's how she treated me—as just another kid who happened to be a little bigger than her.

Our worst fight came on Halloween night in 1998. Steph and the other kids went trick-or-treating around our apartment complex and she came back *without* them. When I asked her where they had been last, her reply was, "I don't know, why are you asking me?" She later explained—while primarily focused on watching television and eating chocolate, mind you—that since she didn't see them, she figured they would find their way home eventually. An eight-year-old and a six-year-old. Um, yeah, that really didn't fly with me. You went back to your room to lie down, as if the night's events were all too unseemly for you to handle. I, however, took a different approach—I whooped her *good and proper*. I gave her a good lecture along with the pops that this was why she had no current privileges—she was irresponsible, careless, lazy, and things of that nature. Her reply was, "Thank you very much for the speech, Martin Luther King." Now while this might have been comical under almost any other circumstance, that time was neither here nor there—so I whooped her again. But she had reached her limit, so she decided to slap me. Big mistake. I had been using my hand, but now I decided to grab my belt. We traded licks for about two or three minutes. After she hit me pretty good (for a young girl) and I could not reply in like force, I decided to end it by breaking her phone. And her homework table. And her lamp. And her radio. She made the mistake of tipping her hand, and telling me she would just use her stuff that she was barred from due to punishment when I wasn't there. My reasoning was that if her possessions were no longer in working order, then she couldn't defy me. Very Old Testament of me, I'm well aware. But it more than got the job done.

As I walked away from the mayhem, she finally broke down the tough façade, and was by then in full on tears. Victory. She screamed out, "You ain't even that smart; you probably cheated your way through college." It stunned me for a second, but didn't faze me too much at the time. However, a few hours later I was a little dismayed. Wow, she really went for the jugular on that one, didn't she? Somewhere around her seventeenth birthday, we began seeing eye to eye. It was a combination of her growing up, and me chilling out. She became less of a nuisance, and I became less of a tyrant. She even started helping out a little—cooking and cleaning and so forth. I began to take more of an interest in her school functions (rides to choir concerts and the like). And I suppose it was somewhat inevitable that we finally came together in our struggles. How could we not, we had been through too much together. We had both seen you at your worse, slept in the same closets, and watched you parade around with guns for days on end when you were going through your delusions. We had both blamed you for many of the shortcomings in our lives. And, at different times, we both forgave you on our own terms, in our own way. The other kids may have seen you at some real low points along the way, but Steph and I have seen it all, and have the frequent flier miles from all those trips to hell and back we took with you. The biggest thing that links us, though, would be that we remember you from the happier times when you were not always sad, or angry, or lost. And I won't be as bold (a first for me) as to say that we're friends now—but we have come an extremely long way from where we started.

Dominique. Bad as hell, and super smart—a wicked combo. That's all you need to know about this daughter of yours. She was a terrible baby, always pinching and biting on Steph. And lo and behold, she grew into a mighty bad young teen as well. She would lie and she would steal. She was mythically lazy—but she was also very clever. By no stretch of the imagination will it ever be said that she always used her best judgment, but after all this time, I guess we've learned to deal with it. One day, I just flat out told her that she is no dummy, and has to be aware of what she's doing to herself. Hanging out with thugs, getting a terrible reputation at school, and so forth. I could see acting like this if she was actually getting away with things. If you're smart enough to pull that off, then you almost deserve to be on the wild side. But she was constantly getting caught, which tells me she's not the criminal mastermind she fancies herself to be.

I was completely honest with her. There would be no 'Dad of the Year' awards on my mantle anytime soon. I know society wasn't built on niceties and a sunny disposition, but instead deception and greed, mistreated workers, and so forth. I told her, "Do what you want to do. You have that right. But if I catch you after warning you, then don't be surprised if I unleash hell on you. That's *my* right." But she knew that last part was mostly all talk. In nine years, I have only whooped each of the kids twice (Cheyenne only once). It just doesn't come naturally to me. I guess I was a believer in the whole time out/ loss of privilege theory that they pushed later on in parenting. Maybe if I had been a little more old-school then, then Dominique would have turned out a little different. Well, you know what they say about hindsight and all.

Now, I wasn't the only one who handled Dominique with kid gloves. Mama Dear and them also gave her a ghetto pass because she was the one who called us when Ray had custody for those two years before he died. Mama Dear taught her the phone number before she left, and every time she could sneak away, she would call and let us know how they were doing, if they were eating well and so forth. She was five-and-a-half-years-old at the time. Like I said, a clever girl, and I respect what she did immensely, too. But, how long can one live off past glories? Especially if her behavior gets progressively worse, and she doesn't even want to pretend like she's going to change? But I think she'll turn out okay. A lot of previous hell raisers/knuckleheads make it. But even if she doesn't and takes an even steeper turn for the worse, I won't forget about the little girl who gave us a lifeline when there was none to be found. Not ever.

Dante. Poppa Doc. Fozzie Bear. The Dusty Man. So many names, he has so *many* names. As you probably remember, they are all based on his appearance—golden brown skin, cuddly face with beady little eyes, curly hair, and a big, muscular frame. He looks like a big teddy bear. And he's my road dog. The only official little brother I've got. There's not a whole lot to say about him—especially on the bad side. Unlike Dominique, he was the sweetest child growing up. So free-hearted and nice. Happy-go-lucky as can be. If I had a nickel for every time I had to pull him out of the street because he was in his Own Private Idaho, not paying attention to traffic, you'd be like, "Bill Gates who? Microsoft what?" He'd just be beat-bopping to the little tune he hears in his curly little head.

Now I did feel a little jealousy for a while toward my boy—I won't deny it. You doted on him, always telling people how handsome he was and so forth. I know for a fact you *never* bragged to anyone in that regard about me, but so be it. I later realized this doting was only because he was still tiny. Still 'your baby.' Once the next one rolled around, that affection would soon shift accordingly.

Not to be cruel, but I've seen it four times now, so I know how it goes. You went from Steph being your darling, to Dominique being your favorite, and then Dante, and finally now Cheyenne. I don't blame you; I suppose it is pretty natural. This is not exactly the same, but it's somewhat like a dog who loves whoever is feeding it at the moment. You're no dog, but each successive baby was feeding you—with all the love you could handle.

The only time Dante ever really hurt my feelings was when he was about eight. I just asked him straight out how he liked things, staying with us, and so forth. And if he thinks he would have liked it better staying with Ray's family. He told me in no uncertain terms that he liked it better over there. *Ouch.* Didn't really see that one coming. I was actually hoping he'd make me feel better about myself and my decisions with his response. I went deep-sea fishing for compliments, and boy did I come up empty handed. I assumed he, if no one else, would give me a vote of confidence, but no such luck. The lesson would have to be that in all my years, I've grown to believe, the truth matters not, just how it's received. But, as I said, I don't have a bad word for my main man. When we moved into our home, Dante helped me all by himself. I'm talking beds, dressers, couches—everything. He was only thirteen, but he's such a strong little dude. He'll walk to the store with you when none of the other kids want to be around for fear that you'll act up and embarrass them. He's always had my back with chores. But little Superman does have one weakness—he's a horrible driver, just like me. Tall, ripped, handsome, and can't handle a car to save his life. Truly, he is formed in my own image. Or shall I say the image of myself in my dreams, to be more accurate.

For the longest time, I'd feel sorry for myself, lamenting the fact that I had no close friends, was always alone, etc. But then I realized that I was so full of it. I in fact knew a guy who never spoke bad about me, always helped me out, and never ran from the struggle. Yeah, maybe I didn't have a friend, maybe I won't have any in the future either. But I will always have a brother—and that's all I'll *ever* need.

Cheyenne. Now when I was younger, everyone would say that I looked just like you. Well, I think I somewhat looked like you, but I know that Cheyenne is your spitting image. Same skin color, eyes, and forehead. She's the youngest—officially your baby, now and forever. Mama Dear thinks that since she's never seen you without your sickness at its worst, that she's actually suffered the most. During the custody case when the kids were taken away, she had barely turned two years old, unaware of the mayhem around her. We didn't get her back until she was four. Janet asked that day if she knew who the lady was who was holding her. Cheyenne's reply, "Mama Selita." How cute is that. Even warms my cold, jaded heart.

After that day, you doted on her to no end. My guess is probably for the same old reasons—with a child who resembles you in every fashion, it's almost like heaping love upon *yourself*. And yeah, you overdid it, as many paranoid schizophrenics are known to do from time to time. I go back to the instant replay of her childhood—no going out, no talking to others in the family, being perpetually tied to your hip and you not letting her out of your sight, etc. It was like a mirror image of mine. See, Mama Dear worried that if you 'truly flipped out,' then Cheyenne would get hurt by sharing a room with you. But what could I do? Having Cheyenne around kept you quiet. And besides, Dominique and Stephanie were pretty damn mean to Shy—in no small part due to the fact that she had your most-favored-nation-status, so it's not like I could ask them to keep a loving eye on her when I wasn't around.

Eventually, I did away with your stranglehold over Cheyenne. I refused to let you monopolize her time, made the other two girls share a room with her, started taking her out on the walkabouts that me and Dante were known for indulging in on early Saturday mornings. And for whatever it was worth, I got Dante's word that he would patrol the block when I was away. My little deputy, if you will. You probably remember him at eight years old, puffing his chest out to everyone saying, "I'm in charge when Manny goes to school." Classic. My real goal is that they would perhaps make a formidable double team to ward off Dominique's tyranny and treachery when I wasn't within earshot.

This just wouldn't be complete and accurate information if I failed to mention Cheyenne's character. Or should I say, *characters*. The girl is hilarious. Always singing, dancing, doing impersonations. She's had so many teachers say that they think she can be an actress—and maybe in a different world she could be. A world where she had her own identity, instead of a Factory Issue #5 for birth order. Where she wasn't the last fleeting attempt of an ill woman to hold onto someone to love. A world where her 'guardian and protector' wasn't too wrapped up in his own drama to notice that she was behind in school . . .

But who am I really kidding with my alternative reality of a normal, healthy, and happy life? This is supposed to be a truthful letter and not a work of fiction, right? Here's some truth for you; how about the fact that I still sleep in closets sometimes . . . after all these years. As they say, you can take the boy out of the crazy, but can't take the crazy out of the boy . . . I take my time getting ready for bed, checking the doors and locks each night. Twice. It's partly for safety, as we have come up in some rough neighborhoods, and the other reason is to ensure that no one can see me, in my shame. It's not every day or every week even. Just something that I do every so often. Birthdays, holidays, painful days . . . to remember and remind myself. I saw Stephanie do it several times before also over the years. As a game, she said. But it has to be more than that, right? A defense mechanism . . . a reminder . . . a reaching out to rewrite childhood trauma and pain? I don't blame you for it, Selita. You thought it would make us safe. Keep us away from the spies, assassins, and evil doctors at the psych ward and juvenile courts trying to take your babies away or whoever else was chasing us in our mind.

Well, again with that truth thing creeping in . . . I don't blame you *now*, I should say. But at first, I did. When you said that you heard people in the attic, and people whispering about you in the house that you could not see, I definitely thought, Oh, she's sick. She's lost her mind. Then Janet said they came to visit you one day at the house and found a woman there, hiding. Turns out there had been people in the house at times. Women whom Ray was seeing on the side. Maybe you had a little help in misplacing your mind that entire time . . . So, this will be the last time, I promise to myself. No more, after tonight. I will act my age. I will put away my baggage in a nice, orderly fashion, in the back of my mind, and not let it peek through that closet door. I will not try to soothe my psyche or heal any old wounds. I will be bigger than my problems and shake my past. Then again, maybe I won't . . .

I am Factory Issue #1—and don't you forget it.

- Manny

December 14, 2004

Dominique got kicked out of school today. And she has a court ticket for a misdemeanor—the whole shebang. Apparently, she and some other girls were about to fail a class, so they naturally decided to steal the teacher's grade book and destroy the evidence of their failure. I know what you're thinking—with a plan as diabolical as this, how could they have possibly failed? Well, one of the girls flipped and turned state's evidence in exchange for lenience. The others—including Dominique—found out and threatened her. And that's a second ticket, right there.

Work does not pay enough to cover this without some other bill being left behind. As Janet would say, "They work me like a Hebrew slave, without the bricks or the mortar," but they don't pay me . . .

I don't know what to do with that gal. She has always been *so bad*. She'll act okay for a little while—three or six months—and then she'll do something incredibly stupid like this. She always says it's not her fault. That teachers are 'picking' and 'lying' on her. Yeah. That works for you— but I have all my faculties about me, Selita. You have to quit coddling her.

It looks like I'll be dropping her off and picking her up from an alternative school every day next semester as there's no bus service from our house. Another great Christmas for your kids . . .

- Manny

February 27, 2005

Jamie Foxx won an Oscar. Wow. It was one think when Denzel and Halle won, as they have been actors from the start. But he has come so far. From doing standup, *In Living Color*, to singing and playing piano. Now *this*. From a small town in East Texas, and raised by his Grandmother too, just like me . . . It's one thing to dream big, and it's an entirely different thing to make those big dreams come *true*. For people like him, Oprah, Michael Jordan, Tiger Woods, Beyonce, Jay-Z, Denzel, Will and Jada, Puffy, I wonder, really deep down, even though they work extremely hard, and believe in themselves to no end, and are aware they are multitalented, shrewd, lucky at times, and of course eternally blessed, if they ever *really* thought they could make it at this level, for this length of time? And if not, how close they might have ever come to giving it all up, and stopping at some other rung on the ladder of life, success, ambition, and personal fulfillment . . . Do they still have those moments of doubt when tens-of-thousands of people scream their names, or they see that humongous balance in their bank accounts, or they collect another award or accolade from their peers and critics? Or are *those* in fact the most trying moments of all, when they fear their tenuous grips as masters of their respective universes all slipping away, memories of where they came from, and the struggle it took to climb that mountain come flooding back in a rush? What keep them going—knowing that they made it, or knowing how hard it would be to try and make it again if it all falls down? I suppose I'll have to make it big myself one day so I can ask them first hand . . .

Till that day comes.

- Manny

April 9, 2005

Here we go again. There's no food in the fridge, and I'm in between pay checks. But when I try to take you to the store, you say all they need to eat is *crackers*. And just to make sure I have this perfectly correct—you do in fact have money, but you're going to let your anger at me prevent you from getting groceries for your kids to eat good meals. Another rousing appeal for 'Mother of the Year' if I've ever seen one.

I am so tired of your games—and just in general, tired of *you*. Since you've been back from the hospital this last time, you have simmered at my presence in the house. Yet, you are well aware that there will be no more refusing to let me in, and no more keeping the kids away from their family. The house, the car, the washer and dryer even—all are in my name. No more threats of running away with the kids to a homeless shelter. You could try to push me if you wanted to, but I'd push you right back, harder— into the system, that is. It's either you learn to live *with me*, or you leave *without them*. No middle ground, no discussions. Basically, I have established that they are my kids as much as they are yours. And furthermore, I would have the tie-breaking vote in all decisions, seeing as how I'm not the one off his damn rocker (relatively that is). I told you that if this was unacceptable, and that you should 'give me his name.' And you looked at me with a puzzled expression and said, "Well, what name would you be talking about, Manny Williams?' And I replied, "The name of the guy who's standing in line to take care of you and all your children the rest of their lives. (I had been waiting six months since our last big fight to use that line). You were silent, and I was content.

Still waiting for that name.

- Manny

October 26, 2005

Astros officially lost the World Series tonight. I knew it was a stretch to win, but did not think they would be swept. All the games were close. They needed Jeff though. He was hurt, and only had a couple of at-bats the entire postseason. One year late, because last season he killed it in the playoffs. To be so good, for so long, and finally make it to the 'Big Dance' and be hurt, that's the worst, man . . . I feel so bad for Bagwell, Biggio, Berkman, Lidge . . . Wanna say there's always next year, but I don't think Bagwell will be back again.

Remember back in middle school when I won some tickets to a game in an essay contest on "What a Drug Free Society Would Look Like," and we went to the Astrodome with Aunt Olivia as my invited guest (which pissed you and Ray off thoroughly). It was awesome. Seats were way up high, but baseball is my jam, and it was my first professional game in any sport ever . . . Ray even bought me an autographed team ball from the souvenir shop, which was awesome, unexpected, and remains one of my prized possessions to this day. Not too many great memoires growing up, but this is definitely one that you helped create . . .

Much respect for all he has given to the game and his fans. Mind, body, and soul . . . And for him and the team making these kinds of moments possible for a kid like me.

- Manny

September 31, 2005

It's been a while, Selita. I've been out of town training my new job. All the crazy storms the last few months, Hurricanes Katrina and Rita, I will be do insurance claims for them. Business and Loss of Use to be specific, for commercial places. It's called Crawford & Co., and they do contract work for State Farm and other agencies. So, for example a Boys and Girls Club had their roof collapse, I handle that claim. Windows damaged at a church, that's me.

We are training in Atlanta. My first time out here, and it is interesting. It's a lot bigger than I thought, with its business district and suburbs. And the airport was both humongous, and super busy. Have not had a chance to see much of the city. One guy in my training class, Karl, is cool. Wants to be friends, but as you know, friendship is not really my deal. Another guy is a new college grad that actually is the grandson of one of the founders of the company. Super Republican, frat boy, bro-tastic. Showed up to the first day of training in shorts and slippers. If I did that, my black but is *bouncing* out the door. He does it, and it's all good in the hood.

He gave us a ride from class yesterday, and we stopped to get Mexican food. Karl was enamored by his Range Rover, fraternity life, fancy watch, etc. It's okay to be in awe of money, but you have to at least *pretend* that you aren't. 'The Chosen One' quickly caught on to Karl's fawning over his life, and it got *ugly*. When Karl asked how much his watch cost, he basically sneered at him. I tried to give Karl the 'cut it out dude' look, but was too late. Rich boy then gave an impassioned speech about how, "Material things don't mean anything to him." And that sure, he had no student loans, and a Range Rover (that he went out of his way to tell us was *used*—yeah, I checked, two years old with 30,000 miles—a true man of the people) as a graduation gift, and his watch (birthday gift) cost more than many people's salary (25k), but he didn't care about that stuff. It didn't mean anything to him and, "Was not the source of his happiness." I love when rich folks tell you how they don't care about being rich. Let's trade then. I've been poor all my life, I'd love to give the other side a twirl. This guy wants us to think he's noble and a good person, and that his head start in life had nothing to do with his current status in life—because he also desperately wanted to believe it himself. Poor Karl. He was heartbroken. I turned down a ride back to the hotel on behalf of both of us. We had an unhealthy number of tacos and elote (Lord I love that spicy corn) after the man-child left, and then walked back on a freeway bridge type thing, kind of dejected, extremely bloated, and doing an extremely poor job of keeping our balance.

- Manny

October 30, 2005

This job is *horrible*. Well, at least it was at first. I drove all through the Southeast talking claims. From Burger Kings at Lamar College in Texas to retirement homes in Gulfport, Mississippi, to machine shops in Mobile, Alabama (where all they had were chicken houses, churches, and pawn shops I swear) and the boondocks of Louisiana, where Karl saw firsthand, and showed me pictures of a call he was assigned with a nursing home covered in blood, and bloated bodies from residents trapped in the flood water . . . I have gotten lost, and had my vehicle broken down numerous times on the road, and got sicker than I ever thought possible, you name it. I was once taking calls during a biblical storm in Pensacola, Florida and was down and out to say the least. I had no hotel, even less money, and had to call Mama Dear collect to ask to get some funds wired. Aunt Lynell came through like a *champ*. Wired me money. Even bought me a cell phone, and had it shipped next day. I sat/dozed in a Waffle Shack all night till that phone came and her money came through and I was able to get funds to drive back home.

And the reason that I was so broke that I couldn't afford to drive back home? The company's payroll was two pay periods behind. No one was getting paid, and people were furious. Cursing out managers, stealing computers and office supplies in 'trade' till their checks came, threatening violence, you name it. Wonder if Mr. Frat Guy had these same concerns as the hand-to-mouth living field staff that his grandfather's company had slighted?

- Manny

❧

November 11, 2005

It's Dante's Birthday

We all went to Mama Dear's for dinner, and we had cake and ice-cream. You chose to stay home, as usual. Mama Dear found something today in her curio cabinet (I think that's the name) that she wanted me to have. It's your salutatorian speech from when you graduated second in your class in high school. I might take a look at it later. Who knows, maybe I'll learn a thing or two about you from reading it that I thought I already knew.

Till that day comes.

- Manny

December 28, 2005

"What's the matter Mary Jane, had a hard day?" That line comes from an Alanis Morissette song, and it's became a running joke between me and D.J. whenever I saw he was down. I asked him once after a rough day, and told him not to worry, because I would, "Place the don't disturb sign on the door." Later that day I played the sone for him, and le caught the lyric and laughed uncontrollably. He is stubborn as all outdoors. Loves to watch TV and movies even more than me. All about sports, loves women, and food, in no particular order. Pre-dispositioned to outrageous temper-tantrums and bouts of jealousy over the *pettiest* of things. I have almost all the same qualities, so of course we don't get along at all. Well, that's not entirely true. We have our moments where we are the best of buds. See, D.J. never really cared for me when I was younger. He was always the first to call out Mama Dear for 'babying' me, and not allowing me to act my age. But I would give it right back to him just as good as I got. He once remarked that I didn't know this or that about football, and I responded back to him that for someone who had his glory days playing high school football many moons ago as an overweight senior on a B-level varsity squad, he sure had a lot of big opinions. I was eight. He wanted to throttle me for that (deservedly so). All nonsense aside, he actually was I think 2nd team all-district on a really good Aldine High School team (football powerhouse), and if it had not been for blowing out his knees, he most definitely would have played college ball on a Division 1 or 2 level at the least. He's only 5'11," but to get on Varsity they needed him on the offensive line. He then put close to 300 pounds on that frame, as the coach built him up to compete.

Too bad the coach wasn't there to put him back together when his body broke down.

Over the years we have fought on things from *John Madden Football* to use of the phone at Mama Dear's house. But we usually made up within a six-month time span. My big wakeup call came when Mama Dear called me a few years ago to tell me that D.J. was in the hospital and had lost a lot of weight due to a really bad heart. Seems that huge frame had finally taken a toll much more severe than his knees, and now his very life was in jeopardy. Docs gave him six months to live. I immediately got my act together and gave him a call. We now have what I like to term as a 'good working relationship,' where if one of us is about to piss the other off, we merely walk away, stay apart two to three days, and then rewind it back to the start, and try again to be cool the next time we cross paths.

He caught hell growing up for being dark, on the chubby side, and having razor bumps on the back of his neck (barbers with jagged, unclean clippers). He was also a black sheep because he hung out with groups others than black kids, liked rock music (Kiss), and dated Caucasian and Hispanic girls. Now, some of our disagreements ran deeper than the trivial items, I mentioned previously. Like when you once asked him to borrow $20, but you could not give him a definite answer on when you would pay it back. He told you that was simply "Unacceptable and not realistic." Now this comes from the same guy I had once given $80 to pay off a video store bill, $200 for a (girl)friend of his I did not even know for rent, and loaned $500 to his sister to help her put a down payment on a car—and he turned you down for $20?! But let's focus on the better times. Like, when I was down once, and he told me, "Smile, because the white man loves you!" (This was actually painted on the side of the I-45 freeway back in the mid-1990s.) Or maybe how he would go to the mall, have a packet of Post-it Notes with his name and number pre-written on them, and pass them out to girls and say, "Call Me". Now, as I saw girl after girl throw them away, refuse to accept, and give out a demeaning laugh over and over, I finally asked him—what's the point? Because it doesn't look like that even works in the slightest? He said, "Basically only five or so out of one hundred will call. But that's four or five I never would have known. It's all a numbers game Manny." Definitely can't forget when he went up to a super pretty girl and said, "Ma'am I'm sorry to bother you, but I just have to say you are without a doubt the most beautiful woman I have ever seen. And I have to ask you, if you are in love?" She politely smiled, and thanked him, but said that she was sorry, but she was married. His reply then was, "Oh, no. I didn't ask you if you were *married*, I asked you if you were *in love*." Oh boy. Mind Completely *Blown*. How could he do that? How could he say that to a complete stranger? How could he . . . make her blush. Then laugh. Then give her that phone number as she walked away, glancing back at him in a flirtatious way. It's all a numbers game, indeed . . .

He has had to fight for everything in his life—from money, to love, to he and his sister's own safety. Just like me, but worse. See, D.J. is also the oldest, and looked after his two sisters and mother as the de facto man of the house when his pop split—but I know his was a much rougher road back then, based on the stories I hear about his childhood . . . Horrific physical abuse from boyfriends of the worst order. So bad that granddad had to go over on more than one occasion with guns and threaten to kill these men for what they did to D.J. and his siblings . . .

But enough of that unpleasantness. How about the definitive, quintessential D.J. story I will never forget? This story explains why no matter what dirt he may pull, I'll continue to give him a shot later in life to be friends again. See, this week our lease up. I initially thought we were going to move into a nice apartment on FM 1960 close to State Highway 249 and Willowbrook Mall. Yet, according to the apartment manager, the leasing rep gave us the 'wrong quote', so even though it was in writing, they would not honor that deal. Well, no biggie, right? I'd just tell her to go to hell and we'd return back to the old apartment. Then she threatened to sue me because, "I had a contract." A wrongly worded, false advertising-type contract no less, and she refused to return my deposit. Well, the thing is, I found out this afternoon that they had already leased our old place to someone new, and they had no vacancies. There we were with no place to go, everything we had was in a U-Haul truck in front of our apartment, and the kids were hungry. D.J. told us to go to his sister Brit's house. He bought us some KFC. And while you and the kids watched TV and dined with the Colonel in the back, I snuck away and went back to our old apartment. I sat in the kitchen with the lights off and cried to myself. About thirty minutes later, DJ pulled up all of a sudden and asked what the hell I was doing, as he found me laying in the bed. I told him I couldn't do it—not anymore. That it was just too much for me, all the lives that I was responsible for. His response was swift and immediate. He told me to stand up. When I shook my head no, he then *stood me up*. He said, "Manny, I know this is some scary, scary stuff you are dealing with right now, but you gotta pull it together. I know you can make it through this." I was like, "Oh really, what gives you that idea?" His response was that that he had always thought I was smart and funny, but the stuff I was doing for you and the kids had earned me his *respect*. I needed to, "Dry my face, wipe that hurt away, and get back out there and find us another place to live. *Now.*" And even though I'm pretty sure he stole at least a portion of that speech from an old sports or war movie, there is *Nothing* anyone else could have said to me, that was more needed, at that particular point in my life.

He has no idea how inspiring those words were. Because right before his Academy Award winning speech, I had taken about twenty-four pills tonight in a second attempt on my life. That's why I really went off on my own, away from everyone else. I wanted to slip away one last time, and be all alone—just the way I felt I walked through life. They were mostly Vicodin (20) and the rest were Tylenol sleeping pills, I believe. I had begged Mama Dear into giving them to me over a period of time. I have had constant pain from my surgeries, to this day, and I would ask her for them periodically. But then, I started just asking for them at will—in pain or not. I asked Brit and D.J. to let you and the kids stay the night, promised I would start the house search in a bit after I took a nap, and I went back as he left, not sure if I would ever wake up. I can never tell anyone about this attempt. They are so proud of me for getting us into a nice neighborhood and sticking up for the kids . . . I just don't want to let them down again . . .

How did this begin? Well, I started to feel unbelievably bad about myself. The house situation was catastrophic, yet it only compounded everything else. My solution was to take two Vicodin. And then I took four more, and so on. I then tossed in a few Tylenol, and I washed it all down with some good old Nyquil for good luck.

I thought my heart would explode upon impact, but all I turned out to be was super tired. I have slept for like eighteen hours off and on now, and have been writing this letter in small doses of lucidness. I guess I have built up such a tolerance to Vicodin over the years—I've taken ten or 12 at a time before for severe pain—that they just didn't faze me anymore. Again, I don't think suicide is a terrible thing, but it can be terrible for those you leave behind.

As I jump in the shower, to try and wake myself once and for all, I imagine that I don't want to actually die, because there's really no such things as an 'unsuccessful suicide attempt.' If the first course of action doesn't work, you do something else. Immediately. If I really wanted to be dead right now, I would be. I realize that. I'd take more pills, or some other action. I also realize what I truly want is for my soul to stop hurting so much. And there ain't no course of action that I am aware of for that ailment . . .

When I think of all I might miss—the kid's graduations, getting married, having children of their own, Mama Dear—I feel really, *really* lucky that I failed at one more thing . . .

Tomorrow, after I finally have my head on straight, I will pawn everything I own (including my class ring—sorry Janet), cash in a few questionable checks, get a couple of high interest payday loans, called in a ton of IOUs from every family member and friend I can round up, and hit the streets running. I will find our next house, I will stop feeling pity and quit harming myself, and I will ~~tell~~ try and be the best me I can be . . .

- Manny

January 22, 2006

Kobe. Kobe. Kobe. I know you were complaining about me screaming like somebody died last night. Sorry, Not Sorry. But Kobe put up 81 points against Toronto. Many of them on Jalen Rose, who I really love from the Fab Five Days at Michigan. A couple of weeks ago he had like 62 against Dallas–in only *3 Quarters*. Never thought he could top that. Shame on me.

Unstoppable. Legendary. *Vicious.*

- Manny

February 26, 2006

You know that I've been working at AIG for a while now, right? You've seen the bag, washed the company sweat shirt for me, no? It's pretty cool. I work on retirement accounts, so sometimes cranky old people call in. But the real worst ones are the financial advisors who actually work alongside us. There's this one named Steve, and he was so mean to me. I'll get him one day—and his little dog too.

One trainer named Robert is cool. He went to UH as well (10 or so years before me), so we talk about that. He's like a Ned Flanders/ Tim Taylor/ world's greatest dad type of guy . . . Does Boy Scouts with his kids, band, sporting events, builds decks with them, and can cook anything in the world in a Dutch oven . . . The kind of dad every little boy dreams of having growing up.

But it's another one of my trainers that I really want to talk about. Her name is Mary, and she has almond eyes, and kind of reddish/purplish hair. She about seven years older than me is unbelievably smart (lived abroad in France, straight A's at Notre Dame, I think), funny, and *loves* music, TV and movies just the way I do, and we talk about all things pop culture vie email at work all day long. Definitely one of the best people I have met in years.

\- Manny

May 24, 2006

Lynell (your younger sister) gave me a $500 check for my birthday. I initially thought it was a mistake, like she missed a decimal point. But nope—it was correct, and it came with conditions. She told me I had to spend it completely, with no exceptions, on only *myself*. Guess it was for me doing a lot for others and not much for myself. Did not see that coming. So nice, and so unexpected.

She has always been super good to me, and all the other younger people in the family. Road trips to Austin, invites to other cities she lived in (Richmond, Olympia), helped with school work, fixing my hair when I had braids, you name it. She is one of the success stories in the family. Good degree, good job, married (now divorced). Chris is her oldest son, and Matt her youngest. Chris is tight with Stephanie. Good-looking kid, runs track. Spoiled though, for sure. Matt was born premature, and was the size of a *pocket comb* when he was born. Takes him a while longer than others to do some things, but he goes to school, plays basketball (travels his butt off trying to do those *And1* moves like The Professor and Skip 2 My Lou), and loves girls and rap videos. Nothing wrong with that boy at all. Matt once had a teacher when they were in Virginia, and she let it slip when introducing herself to the class that she was from Louisiana. Matt instantly asked her, "Ooh, are you from Hollygrove like Lil Wayne"? "Hell, no," she shot back. "I am *not* from the ghetto, and I graduated from Tulane at the top 5 percent of my class." I could have *died* when Greg told me this story. But again, no shame in being poor, if she was. Johnny Adams also came out of that neighborhood I believe. They called him the 'Tan Canary,' and he sang like the sparrow. *Release Me*, *Reconsider Me*, and *After All the Good Is Gone* are some of the best, and saddest, songs ever . . .

I thanked Lynell with all my heart. So, what did I get? A nice skateboard—saw *Lords of Dogtown* and was inspired—but a huge mistake as I have terrible balance, and I quickly fell numerous times on ramps and broke my right wrist. I also got some roller skates for the kids so they can zip around the skate park while I fail repeatedly to live out my Gleaming the Cube dreams . . . Made groceries as well.

Lynell's gift, as beautiful as it was, was only the *second best* I received. Dominique was waitressing at Pappadeaux the nice seafood place with the *awesome* stuffed crab, and who did she happen to see in her section. Dawn from *Buffy*. Along with her boyfriend, Iceman from the *X-Men* movies. Never would have believed her. But she sent me a pic of all three of them! Says she told her how much I loved her, and the show, and Buffy, and Spike, and Willow, and Faith, and Cordelia. Said she laughed at that, and they were both really nice.

Oh, I also got a keyboard with the gift money, so I could try to play a few of Tupac's songs. Yeah . . . epic fail on that attempt. I was actually thinking about him a lot lately. How he could have been an award-winning actor, president, preacher, professor, civil rights leader—*everybody's everything*. But his life went so off course, so much potential unrealized after getting shot, and then getting in trouble. I spend so much time wondering if he ever really left that jail cell . . . Being the son of a Black Panther, born while his mother Afeni was locked up. Reaching such highs in his life, countless hits, loved by millions, film roles. And it still was a drop in the bucket compared to what all his fans *know* he was capable of. To do so much, mean so much . . . to so many people. Only to end up incarcerated, like so many other men of color born in tough circumstances. To 'have it all', but ultimately have it mean *nothing* when you lose your freedom, and then your life. Yeah, I believe he only truly left that cell when he left this earth, and flew right up into the stars . . .

There's also the Jada factor. To grow up together dealing with extreme poverty and addiction in their family, make their way to performing arts school, and have the nerve to conceive those audacious dreams of being world-class artists with fame, stardom, and a better life, and then to actually *make it happen*. What are the odds? Then, it goes sideways. How does he *not* end up with her? In what world does he ever let her slip away? I know all things aren't meant to be, and of course she found true love, had a family, and has beautiful kids with Will, but . . . got to wonder, how things might have played out . . . If they got together, would Pac have calmed down? Or would he have screwed it up, kept partying, and inevitably ruined the relationship, *and* the friendship, by taking her for granted, or breaking her heart? They knew each other so well, "closer than the hands of time," but maybe that's the issue. They knew each other *too* well. Their strong personalities and wills a little too similar. Had seen each other at their worst way too often. Knew how to hurt the other, in *just* the right way, to make it everlasting. I'm guessing he had that internal debate about ten million times over the years, wondering what might have been. And then I wonder, if I will ever find my Jada? Or maybe I already had, but didn't recognize her, and she slipped away. . .

- Manny

July 5, 2006

I was driving home from the skate park yesterday when I heard Fiona Apple was coming here in a few days . . . I screamed like a little Southern Belle and dang near jackknifed my car on the highway. Now, you realize that she and I have been carrying on a one-sided love affair for the past decade, right? And that I know her lyrics like The Scriptures . . . Wow, I bet that came out mighty creepy, huh? But that's neither here nor there . . . Not sure what I'll do since there aren't too many tickets left, and the ones that are might be way expensive . . . What I do know is that I have to go see her light up that stage.

Thank You, Namaste, And Good Luck

- Manny

July 9, 2006

I saw Fiona in concert tonight at The Woodlands. This has been ten years in the making . . . She wore this kind of a . . . blue-purple muumuu? But I'll let that slide. She looked really healthy—not super thin like in all those pics when she was younger. At certain points she seemed to be crying into her microphone, and she'd just bust out saying stuff like, "Don't Pity Me!" Jamon cracked up, and tons of fans around us gave us the death stare, and I hit him and told him to cut it out. Later on, she started slapping the stage floor with her fist repeatedly, and ran away/hid as the crowd looked up at her . . .

But the music was *great*. These two ladies in love behind us kept on screaming for her to play 'Criminal'—while I wanted to hear 'Paper Bag,' "Extraordinary Machine," and of course, "Never is a Promise." She did all but the latter of the three, so all in all can't complain.

At the last second upon entering, security working the gate informed us that she asked for no pictures, so I had to dump my camera with them. But no cameras were needed, trust me Selita—these are memories that will *never* fade.

- Manny

September 24, 2006

I had to go get a birth certificate today. I needed proof because someone stole my identity, and ran up like $1,000 in charges on my bank account. I filed a report with the police, and now the onus is on me to prove I am legit, and the charges are false. I brought

Mama Dear to the police station with me to vouch for me . . . hand to God. A living, breathing security blanket. I was certain there was no way she'd have let them haul her baby off to the pokey. Not on her watch. Upon arrival, I got a straight O.J. reminder that it's not about race, it's about *money*. The law looked at my driver's license and it went like this:

Johnny Law:   "Oh you live in Champion Forest . . . My daughter lives there."
Me:   "Just moved in, Mr. Lawman."
Johnny Law:   "You'll enjoy it there, son."
Me:   "Thank you sir, and good tidings to you and yours"

Now, if I had filed that same identity theft complaint with my old Acres Homes address in the heart of the ghetto, I'm guessing that the conversation would have turned out *slightly* different. I was there forty-five minutes. Then, at Wells Fargo for one hour and seven minutes, trying to prove that me was I and I was him. Good times. They promised the charges would go off the card at midnight tonight, so I'll be up waiting. But this old dog's been fooled before, so I really have no expectations whatsoever. *Another B.S. Night in Suck City* indeed (a great book, greater title, and the author used to teach at UH).

- Manny

October 31, 2006

I found out that I failed my Series 6 exam today at work. Got a 66, needed a 70. Didn't study a single *second* because I thought

I had it down. Had I passed, I would have gotten a $1200 yearly addition to my salary. I guess I let my pride and hubris derail me once again. We could have *really* used that money around the house . . .

- Mannys

November 26, 2006

I missed the Ben Folds concert tonight because I could not find anyone to switch with me at work. He was playing with the Australian Orchestra. That would have been so epic. But I really didn't have the money to throw away on concert tickets right now anyway. Oh well.

- Manny

December 23, 2006

Last night I found this message in my e-mail. It was from Tam, the kids' sister. I hadn't heard from her in, what, five or so years? Last I was told, she had moved away with a white guy in Tennessee somewhere . . . But anyway, it read:

> Manny,
> Hi, how are you? I was searching M.S. and came across your name in my mind. How are the kids? Please contact me at

my email or on my cell. I would love to know how things are going!

Thanks,
Tam

I read it, and then left it alone . . . out of sight, out of mind. But something hit me this morning. I woke up listening to John Lennon's *So this is X-Mas*, and then, I switched up the game with the random program button, and it landed fell on *Just Like Starting Over*. For some reason, I just *felt* that song. I'm guessing it was his Elvis by way of Liverpool line delivery, but whatever the reason, I took it as a sign to call bygones, and let my long-lost, ex step-sister back in our lives.

We packed up to go to Mama's (you declined per usual). As soon as we pulled out, I gave Tam's contact info to Dominique, and she called. She spoke for a few minutes, then passed the phone round-robin to Cheyenne, then Dante. Then came the moment—Dante said she wanted to talk to me. I paused, then hesitated as I thought about it twice—and then chose my *third* thought. I told her hi, and said that there was no need to thank me, I couldn't believe she tracked me down. And that we'd be at Mama Dear's house if she wanted to come by. I also asked how was Ray Ray, and said maybe he could come by too? And then, just like that, she was gone.

So, we posted up at Mama's, and I waited curiously by the partly torn screen door, jumping every time at the faintest whisper of a car driving by the gravel road. And then about 30 minutes later, they arrived. Tam had slimmed down considerably, and Ray Ray had gotten super tall. When I last saw him twelve year ago, I was three inches taller than him, and now he was about four inches taller than me. It was so strange talking to him and having to look up into his eyes. He told me he hadn't played ball in years, and that shocked me. I would always tell

Dante how masterful he used to be on the court. He said he was doing electrical work down by the old Enron building, still living close to Bear Creek. And that he still loves white and Hispanic girls (Dante cracked up laughing over this one). He unfortunately loved one little *too* much, as they apparently had a bit of blow up which ended badly.

Tam has done really well for herself. She works with autistic children up at prestigious University back East. Said it took a while to straighten her stuff out (ditto for Ray Ray), then she went to catch up with the girls. Ray Ray and I stayed outside in the freezing cold with Dante and our cousin Dreis to catch up. We talked about everything from how we used to go see movies at the old Northline Cinema on his dad's paydays, and then go to the buffet at the Pizza Inn next to it. How we used to play ball all day, every day, and how people only picked me because I was his stepbrother. How we battled over music and video games (Ray Ray refused to pass the controller even when he lost), and how we would never lose contact again . . . Something we definitely did not know to be fact, and could in no way promise to one another . . .

He told me that he and Tam were just kids—and they had no idea what was going on between his dad and Selita. That they were just finding out now about some of the stuff their side of the family had pulled . . . I nodded but remained silent. We stood out there for about three hours. It was just like the old times, except that it *wasn't*. He went to the corner store to get a beer (blew my mind to imagine, my little stepbrother drinking beer), and that left me and Tam. She again thanked me for allowing them to visit. She said when she hadn't heard back initially, she figured she never would at all. She said that they wanted to help out in any way possible (Ray Ray said the same), but I told her we manage to get by. But she kept at it. I advised that was a slippery slope—especially with someone like Dominique. Say that to her, and all she'll hear are cash registers popping off at all the trendy clothes outlets.

Tam said that she and Ray were talking in the car over how we were all just kids when everything popped off eleven years ago, and that out of the three of us, I was the one who ended up taking care of everyone (I countered that it was merely luck of the draw—and I was just a terrible card player). But she wouldn't accept my attempts to deflect. She said I had done a great job at going at it alone and had accomplished so much, and so forth. I told her that they would have done the same and the usual aw-shucks doctrine many use as a self-defense mechanism, but, I couldn't, or let's say I *wouldn't*, let her know how good it felt to hear that from her.

They visited for a good long while, since she would be here for a week (and only makes it to Texas once or twice a year). I offered to bring the kids by sometime to allow them to go out together and she jumped on this. They then set up a play date for tomorrow, and of course this is the first that you are hearing of it because I didn't want any blowups or to take the probable chance that you would veto this (or attempt to).

For the first time in years, I really felt like I did something good, important, and worthwhile, and perhaps that maybe, just *maybe*, I wouldn't have to wait until I got to Heaven to get my crown (I also thought maybe they could help me with those triple college bills I'm going to look at in a few years for the kids).

- Manny

December 4, 2006

Mary at work completely blindsided me today. One moment we're talking about *Dexter* (one of the best shows ever—and like any good dealer, I got her and our coworker Margaret hooked too), and the next thing she says is that she's *leaving* in less than two weeks for a promotion to corporate . . .

- Manny

December 14, 2006

Today was Mary's last day. She's going to train in New York, and then will head over for her a big promotion to AIG's headquarters on the other side of town. Man, I will really miss her. One less reason to show up to work and slave for the man . . . I got her a cool model of 'The Island' from *Lost*, filled with the characters, and it even lights up. You know Dante had to help me put it together because I'm not a handy type of guy. I also got her a card that said something to the effect of, "People may come and go, but friends will never be 'lost' (and I spelled it out sideways in bold font just like they do for the TV show—yeah, I'm a super geek)."

I just hope she remembers her made-for-tv friend . . .

- Manny

January 25, 2007

June Bug passed away early this morning in Mama Dear's bed, no less. D.J. called me. He's the same one who told me about Ray's death. Never answer a call from him in the middle of the night is the moral of that story. By the time I got there, Mama's house was already filled with family, cops, and paramedics. He had just gotten out of the hospital, and was doing pretty bad. He had actually fell and hit is head in while being discharged. The hospital should have *never* released him, but he insisted on leaving. I guess he finally went to his true home . . .

I went to deliver the news to Jamon with D.J. He was *devastated*. Although they had been at odds for over a decade (just like June Bug and I), in the last few years we all pretty much squashed the madness, and everything was pretty cool for the most part.

Janet and Lynell will need help making the funeral arrangements—and coming up with cash. I'll pitch in what I can. He was forty-five years old—but that's still about twenty-five years longer than most anyone expected him to see based on how he lived his life in the streets. Mama Dear was heartbroken and despondent. She wasn't eating, couldn't concentrate, and was terrified because she was the one to find him unresponsive . . .

Here's what I wrote for the service program:

Gone, But Not Forgotten . . .

Heaven's great gain is balanced by our great loss, James reminds me of Dismas—whom you might recall as the good thief on the cross . . . Jesus told him, "Today shalt thou be with me in paradise" after he begged forgiveness for his sins . . . An act that I saw James Jr. mimic, time and time again.

From attending Bible study with his good friend Donald Ray, to doting on his granddaughter Raniya and his beautiful daughter Janae, to finally making peace with his one and only son—finding love not just for the child, but the Man named Jamon. The way he silenced the whispers that many of us hear, realizing those streets were not his true love—but rather his devoted Mama Dear. Are y'all aware of the last thing that my uncle June Bug said? That he wanted to lie down where he was born, to find peace in his mother's bed. Now June Bug had his faults, as many of us do, but I've only heard of one Perfect Man—as I'm sure have all of you. So, speak your memories and sing your songs, proclaim he's gone but not forgotten, while I'll say he'll be never forgotten, and never be gone.

- Manny

February 28, 2007

We are moving one more. You should be able to read all the signs by now. Garbage bags aplenty. Utility and cable service men coming by every so often. Wish I had a choice, but we have to go. Me and the owner I'm renting from are not seeing eye to eye on several things. I'll try to get us into the best place possible. That's as much of a promise as I can make right now, Selita.

- Manny

March 7, 2007

Saw the Chili Peppers again tonight. This time was even better because I went with Jamon. We had nosebleed seats, but that's okay. Sat next to a young couple; they were super friendly and were actually burning an electronic copy of the concert while we sat there listening to it. The future is here.

I know they have a new album to sell and all . . . but they neglected *so many* hits from back in the day. *Soul 2 Squeeze, Aeroplane, Higher Ground* . . . all left off the play list. And when they refused to play *Under the Bridge* for the encore after the people begged for it, the crowd actually started to boo a little. Still happy we went, all in all.

On the way home we stopped at IHOP by the house, and this cute college-aged, Gap-wearing, well-manicured waitress immediately started in with her sob story of being in college, enduring a slow tip night, having a boyfriend who left her, only getting to use one credit card from daddy, etc. She asked me how I wanted my eggs about twenty minutes into her diatribe. My annoyed response? "*Cooked.*" She looked at me puzzled, and Jamon burst out laughing, which caused me to laugh as well. Then, she kept on pulling at our heartstrings, working for that tip. She was saying how cute Jamon was, how smart I seemed—I told her she "was super insightful, having known us less than half an hour, and that I was sure we would be lifelong acquaintances". Jamon added the Kelly Clarkson line, "Some people wait a lifetime, for a moment like this." Again, the laughter erupted. Come the end of the night, after we'd paid the check and she was ready to cash in on all the goodwill with the greatest tip ever, we looked at each other with a secret glance, both knowing and not knowing what would come next. Smiling mischievously, we dismissively tossed her two pennies over our shoulders and said, "Para tus ninos," as if she was a ragamuffin street urchin rather than a down-on-her-luck coed. She didn't even have kids, but the line worked. All she could muster from the confusion was, "Hey!" We then took off, running into the night. At this point, I forget whose idea it was to toss the pennies, and who said the line. Sometimes I remember it one-way, other times I remember it another . . . A shining moment in my existence? Probably not. A fun time we always laugh at? Without a doubt.

- Manny

April 17, 2007

Driving home today, I saw you walking from the store and tried to give you a ride—silly, I know—as you never accept them from me. Figured it was because you were mad at me, wanted your space, etc., but I never actually asked all these years, until today. Your answer: "The benefit of the appearance of exercise is fundamental to the appearance of African American women." Hmm, well said.

By the by, It Smells Like Easter Spirit! We went to Mama Dear's house for the holiday and decided to have an Easter egg hunt for the little ones, right. However, Miss Lauren Ashley—Brit's little girl—decided the night before to get a jump on the festivities. She went on to hide about three dozen eggs (raw, mind you) before her Saturday night bedtime. As of my last check this morning, they were still finding eggs everywhere—in the bed, washer/dryer, and so forth. But the best part is, in most instances, they could be *smelled* before seen.

I hope you had a happy Easter sitting at the house watching TV, Selita, because mine was rotten. *Literally*. Karoyce (Naseana's oldest, and a super smart little girl who speaks Japanese, draws, and goes to a Magnet school in the Northwest) was down visiting with Olivia, and we laughed and laughed, until we had no more laughs left to give.

- Manny

May 31, 2007

So, Lebron . . . Always knew he was good. But never got swept up in the whole 'Next Jordan' thing. Super impressed how he came up rough, made it out, and brought his friends along with him to be business partners.

But forty-eight against the Pistons in the playoffs tonight. Twenty-five or so *straight* in the fourth quarter—against one of the best defenses *ever*. Yeah . . . maybe he is *that guy* after all. And perhaps there is a little room left on the bandwagon for me.

- Manny

June 5, 2007

Hey to you, Ms. Lady. You had an interesting day at Fiesta today. You got into it with the checkout girl because she, "Touched your grapes in an inappropriate manner." She looked at me, I looked at her, and we both burst out laughing. She was a cool Hispanic girl; somebody else may have caused huge scene with the manager, but old girl has been around a bit and can shrug it off when someone is tripping. Thank God for small miracles, right?

Talk to you later.

- Manny

December 31, 2007

I quit AIG today. Long story, but here goes. Margaret, and her friend are quality coaches, and in doing so review my calls . . . and they contain screen capture. They saw me online at Match.com. Nothing offensive, no vulgarity, no inuendo, nothing. Just e-mailing a girl I met named Carrie, and getting to know her during down times between calls. One of them took it to the Jr. V.P. He said how *disappointed* he was, that if it had been anyone else, he would let them go immediately, but would just give me a stern warning. He could not believe the same young man who wrote an unsolicited proposal on a redesign of the flow for the company's messaging system to save time and be more efficient *"could do such a thing"*. Like I was the Unabomber or something, man . . .

I felt *grateful* to have my job still, then *embarrassed* that everyone would know. And then *furious* that I was being made an example of. While other people dropped calls on purpose, hung up on customers, took nonstop breaks, I did excellent work. I was a great team member, so much so that I was routinely begged by leadership to take my Series 6 and 7 exams again to become a licensed advisor, and I was without fail a top 10 percent performer with some of the best stats on the floor, month after month without fail. My only crime was that I was *lonely*. And I was now being punished for that. Not the advisors with coke problems, or the agents whom HR found racist messages in their e-mails, or the married workers having open affairs on the call floor, but me. So, I quit. And now I have to get back to the grind and plot on my next move. Can't be out of work for long, as too many people rely on me. Wish me luck.

- Manny

January 1, 2008

New Year. New Me. I have a *great* opportunity to become an Air Traffic Controller. They make huge bank, no pre-existing skillset or experience needed. Just a few tests and a series of interviews. I can do this. I'm pretty good at tests, found a study guide at Barnes & Noble, and am *highly* motivated. This is life changing money, and a real career, not just a job. If I can pull this off, I'll be expecting a parade through the streets.

- Manny

March 12, 2008

I sent a preemptive email to avoid a break up with Carrie, the girl I have been dating that I met online. She is acting mad distant and I am pretty sure she has 1 ½ feet out the door already . . . She will talk to me one day, then be silent for a week. Hang out with me two days in a row, and then not even return a call or e-mail for another week . . . Well, here goes:

> Carrie, I have had the most *Magnificent* week of events occur in my life—but they seem like empty achievements without someone I care for to be there to share in them with me . . .
>
> I apologized to my granny for overreacting, and I spoke with my mother. I took her and the kids to the movies and out to eat, and I told her she could continue to stay with me until she got back on her feet.

But I think it solidifies my earlier idea before she even popped up to let the kids (and now her too, I guess) keep this house as I get one of my own. It's time for me to move on with my life—while still owning up to my responsibilities/love for them. (I looked at two lofts downtown as well—man, they are *so* expensive, but beautiful, close to everything, and extremely cool.

Just like you said—I realize that I was put on this world in a bond to her, and that will never change. Even though she infuriates me sometimes, she's still my mother, and deserves my kindness, no matter what . . .

This is the best she and I have communicated in probably five or six years, and you making me soul search last week as to not letting her change who I am despite the things she has done to me/will do in the future was the spark plug for it . . .

I know I have to forgive her if I want any chance of a normal, happy, and whole life with another woman in the future. I don't *hate* her, Carrie. I hope that's not what you took from our talk the other night. It's quite the opposite—I've always loved her severely. It's just that I always hold out hope against hope that she'll return it—and when she never does, it hurts unbearably, and I retreat away and put up a front so as not to get hurt again. But it's something I'm working at . . .

I scouted some cats at Humane Society and SPCA. They say that is like a three- to four-day process. I just looked online, so I will go on my day off next week. I still like 'She Who Shall Not Be Named' for a girl's name. But I'm also seriously considering 'El Diablo Negro' if it's a black cat. One of my nicknames (long story), and it works on many levels. They have two super chubby, off-white looking cats I adore. If a boy, then it's 'Spike,' 'El Presidente,' or 'El Capitan.'

I got a new car! Well, okay it's used, but still, it's nice—a 2005 Chrysler PT Cruiser. It's Cherry Red with an electric sun-roof, leather and suede seats, tint. MP3 player, the AC blows super cold *and* the windows work, unlike my current ride. I'm riding like a king. I will keep it till August, and then get another one and give this to Dominique for her birthday, I think.

To wrap up, I was so not trying to push/scare you away with my family drama, but that's exactly what I feel like I did. The one thing in this word I did not want. Like I said on my message—you saw me at my lowest point; please take a glance at me at my *best* . . .

- Manny aka El Diablo Negro

March 15, 2008

Beware the Ides of March indeed. So, I am in LA right now. I'll start with that and give you a quick rundown on what I have been up to. I got hired for the air traffic job at the Oakland airport, but I turned it down—just did not think it was fair of me to uproot the kids after all this time and ask them to start over again a thousand miles away from the only home they have ever known.

That's the political answer. The true answer is that I was am bro-ken up over Carrie, and am in shambles. My dream of finally moving to California, gone just like that. After studying for months and acing the entry test, doing interview after interview, psych exam, polygraph, ten-year FBI background check, and heading to LA for final inter-views. And then while here, I managed to somehow lose all my money at Hollywood Racetrack and Casino. *Blackjack Is the Devil.* A word of warning, never double down and split repeatedly. It took less than twenty-five minutes for me to go bust. I started with $300, went up to $425 within the next five minutes, and in the following twenty minutes was reduced to only $2 left to my name, and my tears as I caught the bus to my sad budget hotel with the breathtaking view of the overpass. I decided that was a sign to get the hell out of dodge, and immediately caught the bus to the airport and flew back home. People at the table literally booed me and said I was 'messing up the rotation' with the way I was playing, and the number of cards I took each hand. Had no idea card games are life and death. Definitely see how people go broke, lose life savings, and become broken gambling. It is not for me, at all.

LA is *interesting*. Definitely sunny. Lots of pretty people, but also lots of homeless people. This was shocking, as they definitely don't put that on the postcards . . . For every Lamborghini or Ferrari I saw, there was a homeless man or woman on the street. For every patio brunch I walked by with some group of designer-dressed pretty things, there was someone sitting on the concrete with a sign, begging for change, along with a request for human interaction and acknowledgement. It was weird. You see some displaced people in downtown Houston, but here they were *everywhere* . . .

I'm a mess, and I admit it. I just called the hiring manager and used the excuse that Oakland was not my preferred destination, and that air traffic controllers had some of the highest suicide rates in the country as a profession (up there with doctors, dentists, police officers, and military veterans) as more reasons as to why it was not the job for me. But, at the end of the day, I was *scared*. And I really had hoped if Carrie and I worked out, she might come visit, and even love it (and me), and relocate there down the road . . . Fantasy time indeed.

- Manny

March 23, 2008

So, I have now decided to make a sharp U-turn and dive into another one of the ten million careers I wanted to have before I die—teaching. I applied online, and just found out that I passed the initial round, and will move on to the interview phase. If successful I will gain acceptance into the Teach for America Sumer Corps training program and will teach middle school math this summer in the south side of Houston. It's a great program, and surprisingly competitive to get into. Lots of high achievers come in from big-name schools, with impressive GPAs and credentials. It's like my generation's Peace Corps brother-by-a-different-mother. Many applicants go to impoverished regions with huge inner cities like D.C., Chicago, etc. Then, there are the smaller, but just as much in need (and often neglected) areas like the Mississippi Delta, and Rio Grande Valley in Texas. There are also placements in Hawaii, which is super desired, and you have to be local or have ties to get in I believe. But as the saying goes, 'everything that glitters ain't gold'.

I've been doing a lot of reading about the program online, and it appears that the Hawaii location is not on the sunny shores of stuff ripped out of television and vacation dreams; it's actually super small and poor areas, where some kids are literally taught in areas close to tent cities by the ocean. I guess they have a *huge* homeless crisis there, just like in LA. Makes sense. Not homelessness, that will *never* make sense in the richest, most powerful country in the world, but the location of the largest number of people. Cali and Hawaii are two of the biggest tourist spots in the world. Many came there with the biggest of dreams and schemes, and often they just didn't work out. But they never made it back home, and are stuck somewhere between the dream and the nightmare. Waiting tables instead of acting in blockbuster productions, searching in vain for seasonal (and coveted) jobs at the resorts instead of renting villas and surfing all day as they expected.

Dreams are a dangerous thing . . . but I will continue to have them in spit of that fact. I have a hard time sleeping now more than ever. The thoughts in my head just won't stop. I've quit drinking soda with caffeine, I work out, try to go to bed early and put on music, but nothing helps. All I can think of is disappointments, being alone, have no place or purpose. I don't know what I'll do if I don't get this job. It was *insane* to turn down that air traffic controller career. I have taken now to repeating to myself with my eyes closed that, "I will not try to hurt myself again." I just hope I can actually live up to that promise . . .

-Manny

April 18, 2008

I had my interview with Teach For America two weeks ago, and I just found out that I got the job! That interview was *so* tricky. A group setting where we had to compete against the other applicants. There were essays, sample teaching demonstrations, and then more essays, and interviews, and role-playing. I kept waiting for the swimsuit portion of the competition to be announced next . . .

There will be a summer institute where they train us and teach us how to do lesson plans. We will teach real summer school classes at the back end of it. Then we will test for state certification for our grade level and subject matter, at which point we will then actually have to interview *again* to get picked by one of their affiliated school districts. The voyage has just begun.

I am ecstatic. I'm calling Mama Dear, Janet, Lynell, and Little Greg *immediately*—and then I will surprise Carrie and take her out for the dinner of a lifetime . . . Well, if that lifetime had a $75 limit on his debit card that is.

- Manny

May 24, 2008

So, perhaps Carrie will be my 'Lady in Black' . . .Seeing as how she did not even call, send me a card, or do anything to acknowledge my birthday, which will officially be over in the next 30 minutes. That hurts *so* bad. I care for her so much, and she can't even be bothered to acknowledge me.

I will of course have to check, but I am almost certain both Shakespeare and Lord Byron wrote about the woman they loved deeply but could not have, and gave her a title of that nature . . . And then there's Dulcinea, whom Don Quixote makes out to be more than she is, and sees her through rose-colored glasses. He thinks she's beautiful lady of high society, when really, she's just a peasant waitress or something . . . Now of course there's always *inner beauty*, but you get my drift.

Selita, it is just so unbelievably hard to know I will *never* be the first choice for anyone—but a fallback plan, a place holder till a better guy comes along. I have so many versions of the "it's not you, it's me" speech over the years that I can sniff it out from a mile away, no matter what guise it may take . . .

And the old, "you are perfectly loveable, just not loveable for/to me" line she threw at me last week. I have dated my Dulcinea for six months, but she has never called me her boyfriend. Never let me in .

. . It's like the movie *50 First Dates*. I am always starting over with her every time we hang out, having to prove myself over time and again. As she searched for some inconsistency, foible, tick that could justify her keeping me at arm's length. I only looked for the best things out of her—but she only looked for the *worst* things in me. She dated some bad guys before—I won't go into details—but suffice it to say if these kinds of dudes came around one of my sisters, they'd be *dead*. She told me how they hurt her, and how she wanted a good guy to 'sweep her off her feet' and that she was not interested in that type of bad guy anymore. Well, it turns out she was also just not that interested in me . . .

- Manny

June 9, 2008

Well, I went to see Carrie today after she reached out to me. The one that got away . . . Or is she the one that *escaped*? Ostensibly to say hi, but we both know it was really a *goodbye*. She said that she was sorry for not contacting me earlier—that she had a lot on her mind (work, accident where she severely hurt her thumb—yet only told me of it two weeks later). Oh, and that she was in Seattle camping and backpacking with friends on her vacation. She said she had other stuff weighing her down too, but that it was a really long story. I told her to please go ahead and explain because she had my *full attention*. She said that she just felt really lousy lately. I replied that it seemed to be a rather short story to me. She shrugged at this. Guess the humor was one-sided on that one.

And then on cue her brother stopped by, as they had a plan to watch movies that night—though she of course told me on the phone it would be a good time for us to talk about some stuff. Seems her plan was to have him there to move me along, and her excuse as to why we could not talk longer. Well played, indeed. Nothing against him at all. Nice guy. He actually liked me, her mother liked me, so did her mother's boyfriend and her coworkers. Everyone but the one person who counted . . .

In theory this is point where at last, I finally get over her . . . Well, that would be a lie then. Because, Selita, I hope she finds whomever, or whatever it is she is looking for out there . . . Has a great life, and fat happy kids and grandkids down the road . . . But Lord only knows how much I wish that she could have found that with *me* . . .

- Manny

August 30, 2008

I have met some very nice people while doing the summer training for Teach For America. There is a married couple who are in the program together from Idaho. A few soon-to-be lawyers and finance grads taking a 'gap year,' that are on the path to make big money, but first want a service-based career and to give back before striking their riches. I have also met a few cultural tourists. People who have seemingly joined as resume fillers, and openly discuss with no shame on how it would give them bonus points on their future grad school admission packets and political ambitions . . .

Things were going fairly well. I was teaching 8th grade school math and was lined up for a position on the South side once the new school year began. I had good feedback from the program directors over the new teacher hires, kids seemed to like me. They also provide small stipends and loans for the transition phase, as many teachers are placed in regions outside of their home, across the nation, and face uphill costs in setting up their classrooms. They link people up for housing (buddy system), so you not only split costs, but have a literal in-house support network with others going through the same experience as you. And maybe best of all, they offer a part-time MBA program in many cities, where they work around your schedule with evening classes and reduced tuition so you can get a true teaching license at the same time you do their alternative certification pathway by getting hands-on experience in the classroom. I think it's *genius*. Some critics find it short sighted, them putting starry-eyed young folks out there to 'disrupt' education, without enough practical experience besides the summer training corps, and weekly program sessions throughout the school year and summer. The results can be skewed a million different ways—some huge successes with scores up and some claims of 'teaching to the test.' Some spin-off learning academies for poor students that the community loves and really helps kids, and some claims of forged test scores and stats to make the program look better . . .

And then it happened again. Fear and self-doubt began to set in, you and I were at each other's throats again, and I felt there was no way I could lead a classroom and be responsible for helping to mold young minds when my life was in such disarray. So, I backed away from the teaching commitment. Told them that I had family issues (understatement of a *lifetime*), and that I was unfit to be in the classroom. This was a shocking amount of honesty for me in regards to my personal life. At this point, the story takes a *twist*. Did they yell at me, curse me out, demand that I give back both the stipend and loan the program set me up with? Not at all. They did not shun me or banish me, they instead offered me *another* job. Saw that I had some real-world experience in business (unlike many of the kids coming through), and thought I would be a good fit for their regional office. I could take my own version of a gap year, and then come back and join the next year's teaching corps. My answer—you betcha.

I accepted the staff position with Teach for America as the Development Coordinator, and *really* like it. For the Houston region I raise money, host events, manage the database and accounting for the budget (over $5 million annually and growing), help connect new teachers with donors who will sponsor and mentor them in their new role—including a huge benefit in a few months that will be attended by some fancy, rich bigwigs (yeah, sounds just like me, right?!). There are many ten-to-twelve-hour days, but sometimes I get to go on school tours and luncheons with extremely wealthy donors and meet students. Other times, teachers will bring their best and brightest students or the ones they helped turn around (from poor classroom performance and discipline issues) into exemplary students to show off to the staff—and those are always the best days.

But sometimes it feels like a dog and pony show, parading these kids out, and making them sing for their supper. I mean, the checks have to come in some way. You can only write so many news articles, do so many interviews, without having that human connection. So, we have luncheons, and the benefit mentioned that's coming up with over six hundred guests of oil rich persona, foundation and big-business names, local celebrities like ball players (my new coworker/lead Jessica is super nice and her fiancé knows Shane Battier from the Rockets and says he is a super cool dude. Gotta get an autograph, and points on my jumper!), and Mattress Mac (super rich furniture salesman that loves sports and is always on TV with crazy commercials).

Actually, I met Mattress Mac before in like fifth grade; he came by to do an antidrug speech at my school. It was cool; he gave us D.A.R.E. T-shirts, told us to stay on the straight and narrow, etc.

Looking back, got to wonder if that was entirely out of the goodness of his heart, or some court mandated deal to stay out of trouble? His daughter was on the news maybe five years ago in a piece on having a very bad case of obsessive-compulsive disorder (OCD), and it showed her struggles and attempts to overcome it. You see the money, how he built a training facility for the Rockets, and built tennis complex to get tournaments into town at River Oaks (where I actually went to an exhibition once with Rosalind. Vince young showed up after beating UCS and winning the National Championship, and threw footballs in the crowd. It was wild.) but you don't really know him from afar. You don't know his pain, or that of his child. And what it takes to not only get all those material and career triumphs, but how much even more the cost is to *keep* them. A cost that's played out both financially, and personally. Maybe that kept him away from home. Maybe building that empire from a small lot, to a literal castle that can be seen for miles off of I-45, made him miss time with his daughter, and her disorder could have been caught earlier before it got out of hand. I don't know. And maybe he doesn't either. But I will choose the former path, and make myself believe that he spoke to a random inner-city elementary school, on a random morning, out of the goodness of his heart, and not a court mandated order. And even if that is not the case, who am I to judge either way? And to put a Hollywood finish on the story, his daughter that I mentioned before learned to handle her disease and is at Baylor now, doing great things and helping others do the same as a Psychology grad student and national spokesperson for OCD. Gotta love a happy ending . . .

Be good.

- Manny

September 23, 2008

So, I finally watched *The Notebook*, and must admit I actually liked it. However, the greatest piece of fiction Nicholas Sparks has ever written is on the bio of his website. This stuff can't be true! Karate Champion, Still holds Notre Dame track records, when he sold *The Notebook*, the first thing he bought was a new wedding ring for his wife—and he reads approximately 125 books per year?! Get the hell out of here, man. Guess he was too modest to mention the whole ending the global debt and cancer research he undertakes in his free time . . .

- Manny

November 4, 2008

A Black President? Never gonna happen, pigs will fly first, etc. And now it has happened. President Obama has been elected to be the leader of the free world. The most powerful nation to ever exist. One where he could not attend specific schools, eat in certain establishments, or ride in certain parts of the bus as a child. Only in America. We don't have much in common besides black men in America with huge dreams, wanting a better life for our families, and the world to be a better place. Well, that and a shared love of Blackberry phones, that is.

I am not exaggerating in the slightest when I say that my Blackberry World Edition 8830 *completes* me. It is so powerful, so useful, and encapsulates everything I love about technology. The battery lasts for two weeks at a time. During hurricanes Katrina and Rita no one in the family had reception, no one that is, but me. I could also plug into the computer and project the phone files on to it. Call any country (hence the world edition title), which I did for fun often, even though it was super expensive. I didn't have much to say, and would also ask those that picked up on my random dials the same two questions. Where is the disco? And, where is the bathroom? Any true connoisseur of travel and language will tell you that these are, in fact, the most important and vital questions known to man.

The President elect loves his Blackberry so much that there are rumors he refuses to get rid of it. Political leaders have to talk on certain military-grade encrypted devices that have been approved and vetted for use. And for some unknown reason, Blackberry is not on the approved list. The current most powerful man in the world, and what does his heart desire. World peace? Absolutely. An end to hunger and suffering around the globe? You bet. But above all else—he just wants his Blackberry. As do I. And Puff Daddy. On his TV show, he had *two* Blackberry's, plus two additional batteries charging at all times, and whoa be on to any assistant that let both phones go dead *at the same time*. Now he also employed a guy just to hold his umbrellas for him and open doors, so his priorities are sometimes questionable.

- Manny

December 25, 2008

The Teach For America gig has been an adventure. The person I replaced in my position was super smart and left to take a job in the Texas State

Legislature. She met with me for coffee and gave me some good tips, but that only goes so far. The work is outside of my wheelhouse for sure. I know financials, but the way they document, the database, and tax notices all constitute an *extreme* learning curve. Then you have the shaking of hands and kissing of baby's part of it—the fundraising is a beast all within itself. I know nothing of parties, or mixers, or galas. Just not my world. Nor is interacting with the 'who's-who' of society. The board members are nice enough on the surface, but I can see them judging me with every furtive glare and painstakingly polite smile. From the scars on my head, to my bad teeth, to my cheap suit and even cheaper shoes. When I am taking minutes of the meeting notes when the board gathers, all I can think of is 'one of these things is not like the other.'

Upon coming aboard, my boss gives a big speech on, "How I can do this, we are in this together, rah, rah." Okay. So, I think I am doing good, have my footing, then three weeks into the position she calls me in for another speech on, "How I don't seem happy and she's worried about me?" What the hell?! How I, "Used to dress in suits and smile all the time, and now I dress down, and don't say much." Yeah, I'm swamped in work, traffic is forty-five minutes to one hour—*each way*—from my house due to construction, and I don't fit in the ready-made cliques of people in the office who taught together in regions, and then became Program Directors together. They speak the same language, have walked the same paths, and have known each other for *years*, and, in a way, known each other all their lives because they are *familiar*, and represent the kind of people they went to primary school with, college, and social events. I did none of those things. So yeah, I keep to myself.

But, having said all that, my work is getting done. And I have gotten a ton of compliments recently because I have been hanging in there with minimum help lately. You see, not long after that critique, the boss with the crazy speeches took off and resigned a week later, which in total is one month of me being on the job. Didn't train me, didn't' 'coach me up,' made me locate hidden documents that had not been looked at in months, search for high dollar checks never accounted for, let alone deposited, contact donors that were *livid* on not getting their nonprofit payment records for donations months before I even began . . . you name it. Then there is the walk-in craziness. I see the teachers come in full of life and joy, like I did at the beginning, hopping off the elevator with all the hope and exuberance in the world. Then a few weeks later, I see them getting on the elevator crying after a meeting with their directors, because classroom scores are down and they have difficulty reaching a student base that does not look or sound like them. Because they aren't used to the inner-city way of life, and parents are raking them over the coals, because experienced teachers resent them *and* the program—as opposed to embracing them—due to their worry if this new model takes off their jobs, unions, and way of life, will be in jeopardy. Yeah, I am not the only one who's a little down in the building.

So not only did my boss leave, but she left right before the biggest event of the year, the annual benefit dinner fundraiser (my white whale), I keep freaking about under my breath back home, where there are over six hundred guests, and we are expected to raise a *minimum of $500k,* in order to go take a job leading a private school or something. And in doing so, she poached (or attempted to) a fair amount of our donors on her way out the door, thus sabotaging the program's (and my own) mission to raise funds for the students and teachers. *Allegedly.* Way to inspire the troops, ma'am. The office coordinator called my boss 'The Devil Wears Talbot,' and I thought it was the funniest thing I had heard in a while . . .

So, the Development Department went from a staff of three to an army of one overnight. Luckily, a God-send came my way, a new development analyst named Jessica who is smart nice, reasonable, and helps me out when she can. Seems like we are kind of in this together. And somehow, someway, the benefit went down smoothly. The planning, the vendors, the hotel, the transportation, the speakers, the students . . . It worked. The program people in the office went above and beyond and really pitched in just as I was terrified of it all collapsing. At the benefit while work the door I saw some of the richest, most well-dressed individuals I will probably ever get to meet. One of the women I work with actually has a mother in the U.S. Congress, Representative—Shelia Jackson Lee. She has done more for poor black people in the state and nation than I can write down. She was extremely nice and approachable to all of us, and even spoke at one of our events at an elementary school. Her daughter, Erica, is the Director of Alumni Affairs and a former first grade teacher who graduated from Duke *and* UNC. Super impressive. But she also likes to talk a bit of trash about how great her North Carolina schools are, and this and that about sports and movies. I tell her she may have prestigious set of finance degrees and a fancy title, but when it comes to sports and entertainment, I am the expert. She sits is in the cubicle right to the side of me in our small office, and we are joined by Raven, her smart (and feisty) coordinator for Alumni affairs who is from Chicago, and Stacy, a smart and friendly fresh-out-of-college assistant that is super tall and was a volleyball player, I think.

Then there is Evan, who was the whip-smart and kind Executive Assistant to the Executive Director, and received a well-deserved promotion to become the Manager of Human Assets. She was the main person who initially helped me with board members, showed me the ropes, and told me how to watch myself around the disapproving wealthy eyes. I heard a rumor that she left and married her football superstar boyfriend, who was her college sweetheart. He is the *real deal*, as in top five pick of the NFL draft, Rookie of the Year real deal. Good for them both.

Then outside the office is Julia, a friendly and smart Program Director (her younger brother Ben actually is a college baseball star, and got drafted out of William & Mary). He helps out a bit during the summer, but will be going to the minor league system soon. He asked me to guess what he bought with his signing bonus money. A smart guy, so I figured a condo, and maybe put the rest in a high yield money market account or some stocks and bonds? Negative, this clean-cut, handsome, young white baseball player from a private liberal arts college bought a lifted, tricked out, Chevy Tahoe with 22-inch rims and a booming sound system. *Respect.*

But anyway, back to the here and now. It's Christmas day, and I am at work on a crazy assignment. As I said before, every now and then I rub shoulders with the rich people in TFA's orbit. Melinda Gates came by for an event at a school. Never got to meet her, but heard she was lovely and kind to everyone. Neil Bush, who is one of the President's sons, I met him at a luncheon and went to his home to pick up a donor check. In addition to Senator Sheila Jackson Lee was Senator John Cornyn, who also came by to speak at our school event. Wendy Kopp, the founder of TFA, and Michelle Rhee who is a star in the education world and gets a lot of press, I met both as well, but only interacted with them slightly.

There are donors for the entire organization, and then those specifically for each region. Sometimes I hear some crazy stories from the different regions of teachers who go through the program just to marry a board member's son (or daughter), and strike up contacts of both the business *and* personal variety. Like the old misogynist joke—what's the most popular class of every college girl in the south? Marrying Wealthy 101. In my (limited) defense, I have been told that joke no less than five times this year. In every single instance, it was a girl who relayed the message, I'm just saying.

This brings us to the Arnold family—John and Laura—billionaires with a 'B.' He's from Dallas, I think. Both have impressive degrees and pedigrees. He started his foundation after making said billion before age thirty in energy/oil and gas. They help with education, criminal justice reform, and more. Never met him, but I am outside their gate ringing the bell on the biggest holiday of the year. She is expecting me, and I am ridiculously nervous. They donated $500k through their foundation, but we never received it. Accounting mishap, and they advised we (as in *me*) could pick it up so it hits before the end of the year on our books for reporting purposes. She comes to the door, and is super nice. Kind of shocked, as I expected a butler, or a *row of butlers*, for that fact. But she came up, looked amazing, and had a check book in hand. We introduced ourselves, and then it happened. She gave me a signed, and otherwise blank check to fill out, as needed. Oh. My. God.

All the thoughts went through my head. Could I make it to Mexico? Write it out to myself or 'cash' as opposed to TFA? Could I make an LLC to incorporate, then switch it to a personal account? Could I pull up a credible list of countries with no extradition treaties with the United States, and make it down there and get lost in the maze of the holiday season, getting a few extra days for my global getaway? Offshore Cayman account maybe? Funnel through a South American dictator and buy a small village to rule as I see fit as a benevolent overlord?

As I said, *all the thoughts*. And what do I ultimately decide to do with all these opulent options leading to wealth and privilege at my feet? March my melancholy self and this check back to the office, and place it in the mail for UPS overnight, so that it can make it to New York and the central TFA office for processing before the end of the calendar year.

The little ones whom I am helping close this education gap better love me for this.

Merry Christmas to you all. Be home in a bit.

\- Manny

February 19, 2009

Hey you. Long time, no talk. I have been dating a new a girl also named Carey (spelled different), who told her friend I was not a good dresser and was not stylish enough. Fair enough. She seemed to love the kids, though, and she would cook things for them (spaghetti, cookies). Honestly would think at times that she wants them to be her family, just me not to be her man, and would adopt them away if she could. She is a big dog lover as well, and we go to the dog park and get super muddy with her two little guys. She's training to be a speech pathologist with the city/school system, like you were many moons ago. Small world.

I also went out for a while with Jenna who is older (37 to my 29), super smart and fun. We saw *Juno* together, ate Mexican food, had a few adventures. Her ex is a crazy cop with temper problems. I was constantly looking over my shoulder and felt super nervous going out with her, or hanging out at her place. They make Lifetime movies about that kind of situation. But she is in education too, met Dante at the bookstore and got along well with him, has a great laugh and makes me feel good about myself. So, what is my response? Naturally I broke off things with Jenna to focus on the original Carrie, and then tried to circle back once that ended, but it just wasn't the same. And as anyone could have imagined (except me it seems), I turned my back on someone that really liked me to chase a doomed relationship, and ended up alone as a result. Couldn't have happened to a nicer guy . . .

Down the line, I met another lady my same age named Adrienne who was *extraordinary*. Intelligent, funny, artistic, and kind. The real deal. We dated six months maybe, and had fun, but clashed over the dumbest of things. She wanted to eat sandwiches every day, and I like warm meals. She gave me a Garmin, but I prefer to write out my directions on paper. She's social and likes to attend parties and gatherings, while I like to stick to myself and a small circle whenever possible, and then randomly want to be the life of the party at other times—at my own choosing. Gemini curse indeed. Could have been a right person, wrong time sort of deal. Or maybe wrong person, wrong time. Great girl, though, even gave me a professional recommendation *after* we broke up, which I thanked her for profusely. We broke up on Valentine's Day. Yeah, I have nothing bad to say at all about her. Or anyone really. Things work out, or they don't . . .

On a side note, I may have helped saved somebody's life at work today. I think. A girl named Elise went into distress in the elevator. It had been stuck for a long time, and apparently, she had a seizure. I was standing there when the doors opened, and she screamed, "Finally!" Then she shook for a bit with her fist clenched, and then dropped her designer shades (clue number one something was wrong) and just hit the ground. *Hard.* She started shaking, faming at the mouth, and crying. I put my phone in her mouth (another shout-out to Blackberry) so she wouldn't bite her tongue off, right after I called 911, and I was actually talking to her on the speaker phone *while* it was wedged in her mouth.

Then, when she stopped shaking and also stopped breathing, I cleared a bit of vomit out of her mouth, checked her pulse, and did CPR as the 911 operator instructed. It seemed like forever, but it was probably only a minute at most . . . I thought it would be all dramatic and she would gasp for air, and sit straight up in a burst, but her recovery was slow and gradual, like someone turned on all the lights in her body and then she slowly came to . . .

Elise is doing much better now. The hospital is going to hold her overnight and release her tomorrow. Her boyfriend came up from Conroe. Her folks are all in Louisiana I think, but her boss let them know what had happened. I was scared . . . I did not want to do anything to worsen the situation, but when she stopped breathing after foaming at the mouth, so I knew I had to do something. There was one other person on the elevator with her when the door opened. A girl told me as she stepped out to leave that she seemed to be panicking as the elevator took a really long time coming down. And this lady was a vet tech (we shared the building with them), had her scrubs on and everything, and did *nothing* to help. Couldn't be bothered. I know it's not the same as a doctor or a nurse for humans, but you have to have some kind of medical training for that job if you're wearing scrubs, am I right? Let alone having compassion for someone in need at a minimum . . .

Glad it worked out, but not so glad I had so much work to do once I got went to the work after four hours in the hospital. Back at the office, the girls I mentioned before (Erica, Stacy, and Raven) gave me an ovation. I thought they were messing with me at first, but they swear it was sincere, and called me a hero. Not a bad day at the old coal mines.

Hope your day is going well and is a lot less exciting.

-Manny

P.S. Almost forgot. The way I spring into action during that crazy sequence of events. How I knew what to do, and instinctively helped that girl? It wasn't from TV, or a how to article on the internet. It was from watching *you* do the same thing for a boy that had a seizure at the roller rink by Ray's house back in the summer of '93. By my recollection there were at least a hundred people there, and you were the only one to help. Laid him on his side, belt in his mouth, cleared airway, performed CPR, and had someone call 911. All in flash, with no hesitation. By my seeing you in action, you may have actually saved *two* lives that day . . .

April 1, 2009

So, I am running away from home. My birthday next month will see me turn 30, so I imagine I'd be one of the oldest runaways on record. I left for Dallas today. I know y'all thought I was joking, or bluffing—but I am *gone*. I will try my best to make it out there. I just really need a change of scenery . . . A new city with new faces, and new places. Wish me all the best. It's the least you could do. I have accepted a job with the Dallas Police Department. I think I can be a real factor in helping people, and that's a job that will put me on the front lines.

Elise, the girl I helped at work came back recently. She has taken time off, and is on anti-seizure medicine now I believe. She stopped by to thank me, and even made me some chocolate chip cookies that were delicious. I told her no thanks needed, and I really didn't do much, and was happy to help. She gave me a nice card that said she, "was really scared and did not know was happening, but when she woke up in the hospital room and saw me standing there, she knew she would be ok."

She *almost* got me to cry with that one. Almost . . .

Till the next time we meet Selita.

- Manny

September 23, 2009

I am officially no longer a recruit in the City of Dallas Police Department. To put it bluntly, I did not fit the uniform. I did not fit the culture; I did not fit anything.

My first hint should have been at the panel interview. It consisted of an officer, Sergeant, HR rep, and community advocate/liaison for the department. The liaison was the only black person on the panel, and I hoped she would have my back. Hope was soon dashed, as she was the hardest on me out of all of them. "Why a career change? Wasn't I too old? Too out of shape? What would I do if an assailant had a gun to a woman or a child's head?" She knew, and quickly replied that I'd probably be too scared to act, and would be blown away, and get the child killed as well. *Yikes.*

The sad thing is, I want to help people so bad, I just don't know *how.* Teaching didn't work out. Nor fundraising. Neither did police work. Or financial planning. Or the other litany of jobs I've had since I was thirteen years old, working at the corner store under-age. What can I do? What am I good for? What value do I have to offer anyone? I like to say that I am keenly aware of my self-worth down to that last penny. Right about now, I can't be given away with a free coupon . . .

Sgt. Rosie rode me like Seabiscuit, and had a look of *utter disgust* every time I was in her line of sight. Now I realize she not only was responsible for me, but all the cadets in recruiting Class 315. And if I go out there unprepared, unfit, without my head in the game—I am not only endangering my life, but everyone on the force that I could potentially be partnered with, or whose help I would need if I got in trouble on the streets. Just as the lady at the panel interview predicted . . . Sgt. Chris was a bit more sympathetic, but knew I was a screw up all the same. He had some great stories. One about the 'fight of his life,' where he was duking it out with a bad guy down in a ravine and went off air and they had to send in the whirlybird choppers to go search for him. Cool guy, though he basically played Good Cop to Sgt. Rosie's Psycho Cop.

Then there was Sr. Cpl. 'Bird Man,' the no-nonsense leader over self-defense and training, who was in *magnificent* shape. I swear that Chuck Norris or Sam Elliott will for sure play him in a movie one day. Sr. Cpl. Mike, a former boxer who assisted in self-defense and training, was also big in the union. Playboy type from New York. Both very awesome, but take no B.S. kind of guys. And how could I fail to mention the supremely built Sgt. whose nickname was 'Robocop,' that could tune out *eighty-four* pushups in a row like it was nothing while talking crap about you for not being able to do the same. He had some cool stories on the different precincts, and how South Dallas (where the academy was in a rough part of town) compared to North Dallas (where the rich people were). Down South you could crack some heads, violate some civil liberties (only to get the job done, of course) talk crazy, do some *real* police work. Up North, you were more of a civil servant, who better watch his tone, lest you get a complaint from some society leader upset that you didn't make them proper English tea while taking their statement.

As for the actual recruits, there's Jeremy, a former college basketball star at Arizona State, who was a *great* friend to me at the academy—helping me study, with workouts, and pep talks to hang in there. Corey, a former Cornerback for SMU that blew his knee out but was still a physical specimen and super funny. Patrick was a bit of an aww shucks, good old boy from Ashville, North Carolina, that had my back often, and also gave me a job reference down the line, as did Jeremy. Sean was a chubby dude that could run his butt off, but failed out of class by just a few points on the academic portion of the testing. Kyle was an ex-military MP who I thought was a friend, but in reality, was talking dirt about me—how I was out of shape, not fit for the job, etc. We did the gauntlet activity of being sprayed by mace and having to fight off a defender and give verbal commands. He and the leaders were shocked I made it through, and did a fairly good job, and told me so. Talk about the soft bigotry of low expectations . . .

There was the pretty female officer (who leaders shamed/warned not to fraternize as predatory cops would circle her), who I heard was later recruited to be on the *First 48* TV show that shadowed Dallas officers. Then there was a seemingly nice guy whose uncle was an officer, prior military, was friendly and a good schmoozer, and seemed like he would breeze through. Then he got arrested for a domestic dispute, has his picture plastered in the papers, and was bounced. Did not see that coming. And then the officer who left Hawaii (God knows why) and their version of highway patrol, to be an officer here. I think his wife's family was from the area, and they were moving to be closer to them. And Charles, another former military, older black recruit who was in good shape, and would light up cigarettes immediately after his three-mile runs when the bosses turned their back.

How did I get to this point of quitting? Great question, Selita. I got super sick and passed out during PT (physical training). Everyone thought it was just typical 'Manny being Manny,' and not able to cut it, bit. However, it was no laziness or 'failure to act like a man' this time around. I was unbelievably sick. As in can't move for days at a time, losing twenty pounds in two weeks, not eating, and sleeping on the floor, face down vomiting sick. Turns out the same day that we were maced during the gauntlet, I went swimming at my complex. Didn't notice on the pool, until after I recovered, that there was a notice of being shut down 'due to possible water contamination by the city'. Nice. There was also a staph breakout at the academy, which is a breeding ground for such things, so it could have been that.

And for dinner that same night I had raw oysters with a friend who brought along another friend who was a Russian math or economics lecturer at SMU. The perfect storm. I'm not saying she was a spy that poisoned me, but I'm also *not* saying she was a spy who poisoned me. The truth is out there . . .

Went to the doc and received a Z-Pak of antibiotics to take, and that helped after a while. Told her my symptoms; she said it was a nasty virus, standard fare, but I'd be okay. She asked what I did for the city, and I was scared to respond. Last time I told a bank teller in my neighborhood who helped me set up my account what I did, next thing I know I'm being called out at roll call with my fellow cadets and made to run extra miles, because I was stupid enough to say my profession out loud. Cadets are warned not to wear any city gear, tell people what they do, etc. because you never know who hates the police out there. Fair enough.

But I took a chance and told the doc, and she had a look of sympathy in her eyes. She told me how tough she heard that academy was, and asked how I could do that and put up with the craziness within the department, and wasn't I concerned for my safety, etc. I told her, yeah, it was pretty tough, but that I was hanging in there. *Barely*. And that a lesser man would be scared, but once she checks my x-rays, she will note I have steel forged in my spine, and my blood work will in fact show ice water running through my veins. We both laughed at this as I headed home. I still felt bad, but this simple, kind human interaction made me feel a bit better. A week or so later, she calls and lets me know that it slipped her mind and that she should have gotten me tested for the Swine Flu, as there was a serious outbreak in the city and there was a good chance that was what I had.

When fully recovered, I looked pretty decent. Losing that twenty pounds came at the right time. It helped my running, stamina, you name it. Sgt. Rosie even pulled me aside and said that she noticed a change in me physically and was impressed that I was competing 'given my obvious limitations.' She still didn't know what I was doing there, and was concerned for me going forward. I passed all the academic portions, gauntlet, active shooter situation, driving course, etc. Only a few weeks to go, and I would be an actual officer. And that's when it hit me—I didn't *want* to be an officer. I wanted to help people, but this was not the road to helping them, or myself, and I did not belong in the badge and uniform. So, I resigned. And after leaving the academy, the weight of the world was off my shoulders. Did I keep up with the running two to three miles every day? Do the CrossFit exercises with funny names? Community service to help others? Nah. First official act post-academy was to get a Papa John's pizza, sit on the hood of my car, and eat the whole thing in the parking lot. No meal ever tasted better.

- Manny

P.S. Please tell Steph Happy Birthday for me.

September 31, 2009

I've been pretty sad, lately. Away from home, no one I know up here, and just like clockwork, I quit yet another job . . . Things have really been snowballing lately.

My best friend in the world (and cousin) Jamon is in jail . . . Locked up like an animal for something he didn't do. He's smart, talented, good-looking, and athletic, but he still fell through the cracks and got caught up by the system. He can play the piano, speaks fluent Spanish and some Portuguese, is loved by everyone (especially girls), but it wasn't enough. I think back to all of the conversations, meals, and fights where I hoped his story and mine would not end in tragedy, and yet here we are . . .

Little Greg came down from Austin once to work on our computers. I was home alone, and we were going through specs, log-ins, etc. He got the sound player working and got me some nice little external speakers from the thrift Goodwill computer outlet store (yeah in Austin they have Goodwill's with no clothes and just electronics. *Twilight Zone* territory). He put on *Hypnotize* by Biggie, and at that exact moment, Jamon burst in the door like the law, didn't miss a beat, and started dancing up a storm. One of the funniest things Greg says he ever saw. I didn't laugh though. I was jealous, which I am ashamed to admit. How come *I* didn't think of that? How come I didn't have that effect on people, and be able to entertain and light up a room? Jamon just had that *something* . . . something that I knew I never could or would possess. I used to change his diapers and babysit him (I am five years older), but now he drives me around, takes me to concerts, gives me pep talks about you, jobs, and girls. When I started drama at the basketball court, he backed the guys down who wanted to jump me. When I felt down over my life, he would talk to me, make me watch a movie, or cheer me up. He played the part of big brother better than I ever did for him (though I owned the car he drove around, and paid his rent, utilities, and groceries). But I did it happily, willingly, just to keep him in my life. Sometimes he would fall of the radar for days or weeks at a time. He would invariably be in one of several places—a girl's house, on a 'run' raising hell, or in jail. I bought him a cell phone so he could better keep in touch, but he rarely replied. It hurt often, but in time I accepted when he wasn't with me where I could protect him from his life, and vice versa, he was exactly where he was supposed to be—making *someone else* feel better about themselves, and laugh, and feel invincible, just because they were circling in his orbit . . .

And now, he is in a cage for twenty plus years. I *begged* him to take a plea deal. Walk out of jail instantly. Play it safe. Don't test the odds. Get out, take your freedom, and live to see another day on the outside. He didn't want to do probation. Said he "could never pass the drug tests, and would not be able to go to the club". You can't make this stuff up, man . . . I offered to let him stay with me, told him I would pay his probation, get him a job, please, please, just take the plea and walk out. But unfortunately, he is like me—a gambler—and he bet on himself big and lost it all. At first, I came up to see him two or three times a week. I put money on his books, sent letters, mailed pages I ripped out from sign language books, as these were used as a form of communication that prisoners used to avoid detection by the guards. I took Dante up there a few times to see him to 'scare him straight', and show him what one single bad choice can lead you in life.

I made a big play to get him out. Gave his mom $5k—which was everything I had in the world. I got proof that his frenemy set him up, gave it to the lawyer and the family, and I waited for the moment. The special moment where I was a *hero*, and he was *free*. But that moment never came. The lawyer didn't use the proof due to ineptitude. The plea deal evaporated, and his life was over. Then, in time, the visits became more infrequent. The collect calls sometimes went unanswered. And the memories started to fade. I am not proud of how I disappeared. What I am is hurt, scared, mad, disappointed, and heart broken. It hurts too much to see him that way. I occasionally reach out to the Innocence Project, and other groups to see if they will help with the case, but only assist from afar. It's all I can bear.

So, yeah, I've been pretty sad . . . Anyhow, I reached out from my cave of loneliness to venture on the internet, and though I promised I would never again due to how the first go turned out, and even though my heart told me I shouldn't, and my wallet told me I couldn't, I re-joined the dating site Match. And guess what? I met someone, and it's going better than I ever could have imagined.

She's beautiful on the inside and out, funny and weird, and play-ful, and super smart, artistic, and on some otherworldly dimension—mind-body-consciousness stuff. She like grew up in a strict Baptist family (recently lost her dad) and has traveled the globe, speaks like thirty-seven languages, and most amazingly of all—seems to actually like me, just the way I am . . .

I swore I would leave the online world alone after the hits and misses of last year, but when I saw her, I knew I'd hate myself if I didn't give it the old college try. I have a good feeling, no, make that a *great* feeling about this girl—and I think this could possibly lead 'somewhere.' A feeling that maybe, one day, that I could even tell her about you, and Jamon, and everything else, and she might be able to understand without judging . . .

More positive than I should be, considering the horrible news I just got. Dante was found with drugs at school today, kicked out and went to jail. Luckily Rosalind bailed him out. I drove back to Houston and con-fronted him. Ransacked his room and found weed. Not sure who he got it from, how long he's been taking it, or what. He was such a good kid. And I don't know if I am more hurt that he us doing this to himself, or doing this to *me*? After all I tried to give him and the others over the years. With all that he has going for him, the tools to have a good life. Here he is doing the same thing as Junior, Jamon, and so many other young black men. He had no answers. Not even after I slapped him several times, punched him in his chest and arms as well. No tears, no remorse, no words. Did he like to get high because of his friends? Did he think it was fun? Or did he feel he had to, in order to escape that chaos around him, that I was unable to shield him and my other siblings from? I hope it wasn't that. And just in case it was, maybe it's better that he had no words to give . . . Turns out that not only was I unaware of the drugs, but of numerous things. He wasn't going to school, he quit playing basketball, hell I found out he doesn't even like basketball. He likes football, and only played with me because I like it so much. I had given him a storyline, made him the star in it, without consulting him in the least, and now was pissed that he dared to go off script. And then came the realization of why I was really so hurt, because he was not going to follow the path I chose for him, he was not my lieutenant and proxy to deal with the family while I was off working, because he did not want to be tapped to follow me in my role as guardian and protector for our family, and this was his way of forcefully making me aware of said fact. And in this light, I am not the hero, but the villain. Because I was in fact doing the same thing to him that I resented Mama Dear for doing to me all these years, and was never even aware of it . . .

- Manny

October 10, 2009

Well, I did the unthinkable today, Selita. I think I tricked that girl I met online into really liking me. Let me tell you more about Michelle.

We had our first date/meetup at Starbucks. I sat in the back-left corner. She looks around, and in a crowd of say twenty people, she goes to the only other brown-skinned guy and asks is that me. *Brutal.* Will never let her live that down. I kind of have a face that people don't forget, ya know? Said we must all really look alike—and she was mortified. Told her I was only kidding, but she was still embarrassed.

Well, I guess you don't know her since you've only heard whispers about her over the last few days. Anyhow, we had a great day together (down in Dallas) and she said she was not going to be looking online for anyone else. Without revealing too much—she's been hurt in the past. And I wish, like anyone with a heart, that she hadn't. That I had known her then, and maybe saved the day . . . saved her. But what can you do, right? As they say, "can't change yesterday, but you can definitely alter tomorrow."

I want to defy the odds of existence with her. She said that she wants to find someone she can enjoy life with. That she is 'hoping to meet someone to share in the experience of it all' . . . and that she thinks there's a chance I might possibly be that guy . . . I really am not sure at all why she likes me. What is drawing her in? I'm just hoping whatever false light she's viewing me in can shine just a little bit longer—say the next thirty or forty years . . .

I was telling her how I like to write in my spare time, and dream of one day being successful enough in whatever career I settle in to take care of you and the kids, and especially Mama Dear. And she didn't laugh or roll her eyes. Just merely nodded, smiled, and said that she enjoys my words (though they tend to be sarcastic), and how I use them, and that all I need is a break one day. Her response was simple and straightforward, but truly meant the world to me.

I saw a Brian Wilson biography once, and his wife was speaking of how, after his breakdown, most people pitied him—a great talent laid to waste. A genius betrayed by his own beautiful mind. And for the briefest of moments, she admitted she shared these thoughts as well. And then, one day, she was awakened in the middle of the night to the most lovely song she had ever heard. She went to see what Brian was listening to and was blown away to find that it was him playing something new he had composed only recently.

When he saw her, he stopped. She pleaded with him to continue—and even more so, record it, so people would know that he still 'had it.' But he shook his head and told her, "Nah, that's okay." Why not, his wife wondered? How could he possibly not want to share this with the world? His answer, "Because as long as I know, and you know, that's all I need."

That's what I want most from this world than anything. That's how I want to help people. Beyond money or success, above all else. I want to make something extremely beautiful, and even if no one else recognizes it, I want to know it exists, and I want Michelle to know too . . .

I'm not sure if I completely believe in everlasting love, but I am sure that I completely believe in *her*. When she talks, it's like she knows my thoughts already. Confirming my wishes and dreams, as gaudy as they may seem.

When she calls, I get a feeling all around like I never thought I'd see. As if she sings out a silent prayer—a prayer heard only by me. Gave her a copy of the film *Rushmore* and the book *Dear White People*. She loved them. Or at least she *pretended* too.

But again, I'm no hero. Super vague on my back story, played a few mind/word games with her. Said she took a church trip to China and saw the Great Wall. I told her, "All walls are great if the roof doesn't fall." Shout out to Bjork and Thom Yorke. She was so confused—could literally see the hamster turning in her head. I told her don't fall in love with me—because I will definitely break her heart a few times, and make her cry. Girls *love* a challenge like that. I am a rascal—Rhett Butler style.

Yeah, no hero indeed . . .

- Manny

December 14, 2009

I wrote this inside a card for an early Christmas present to Michelle:

*Try as I may, try as I might, I'll never be seen in your type of light. While I might sometimes overlook the right thing to do, you realize above all else that you have got to live with you.*

*You honestly care and are aware of the choices that I make, and always sincerely listen to me, as long as it may take.*

*I thought meeting a great girl might not happen in this lifetime, Yeah, I've always believed in magic—but I figured it would be really hard to find.*

*Fairy tales are easily led astray, so I refuse to try to classify 'this' too soon. But when your day goes wrong, and you find it hard to move on, just picture me somewhere, cheering you on in that room.*

*You told me there were tough times in your childhood, and life has not always gone as you planned. Well, when it comes to things going more bad than good, and longing to be truly understood—baby, I think you know I'm the guy who understands.*

*I lack the power to prevent darkness from clouding your smiling soul and mine, yet at the end of each day, I'm most certain you'll be okay, due to that silent prayer that traveled from your heart to mine.*

*At the end of the day, I'm most certain you'll be okay. I realize this every time I steal a glance at your beautiful eyes . . .*

*And mostly because while some girls in this world were only born pretty, you, Michelle, were also born kind.*

I'm optimistic, like Radiohead, because I asked her to be my girlfriend—and after reading this, she said yes.

- Manny

December 24, 2009

Just when I think that I have hit rock bottom, somehow, some way, I continue to raise the bar. I have written bad checks for groceries. Taken out payday loans that I knew I could never pay back. Gotten cash advances from checking accounts, then went off and opened new accounts once the payback was due. A 5k loan from TFA that will stay on my credit for seven years. Multiple cars repossessed, including some that I promised to the kids . . .

And what have I done to possibly top all that glory? I am donating plasma on Christmas Eve, just to have money for food, and to buy Michelle a small gift. Well, make that *attempting* to donate plasma, as the center will not see me today. It appears I have given too much recently, and need to wait another day. Once again in my life, my timing is impeccable. And on top of that tidbit, I just learned that there is a sliding scale for payments, where you receive less each time you donate. That's the reason why the money I have gotten has gone down from $45 to $40, and now $30. It's gotten so bad, with being out of work for months, that I had to grab some DVDs to sell—Michelle's and mine—just to have gas money to make for the next few days. Much love to the Movie Trading Company.

I was too embarrassed to call her for help, but eventually swallowed my pride and did. However, she said that she was short until her payday tomorrow, when her check was ready. Hmm, so on to the next option, I sleep in my car in the parking lot of an apartment complex  in maybe the roughest part of Dallas. The plasma center was located about five minutes away from the Police Academy that I washed out of. I'm surrounded by people that I was supposed to protect. People that I was hired to be an example and inspiration to. Now I'm shivering at night in a car with no heater, hoping they will not see me, judge me, ridicule me, or rob me.

This is in no way beneath me. I've slept in my car for the last few months now. But in 'nice' places. Parks, White Rock lake, and so on. I have read in libraries for hours, wandered through Walmart for days, used the same cup for weeks to get free refills at Jack in the Box. But his is somehow different.

I made it through the night with less than an hour of sleep, and was able to donate in the morning $30 as advertised. Score. I make it to Michelle's, with a quick stop to sell the DVDs, and then to pick her up some perfume at Kohl's. It's from the Britney Spears collection, an inside joke based, but actually smelled pretty nice.

I give it to her, and she laughs and thanks me. I tell her I love her, and she says it back.

We are not at the feel-good end yet, though. The next morning is Christmas Day. I wake up feeling the day will be mine, never to feel the same sorrow as the last twenty-four hours. And then while getting some fresh air on the balcony, I see that my car has been repossessed. I had been parking at several of the apartment complexes adjacent to hers, in the hopes that I could get them off my trail. They must have figured it out. Everything in the world that I have was in there. My clothes, my books, my cherished Blackberry.

After I quit Dallas Police I bounced around, looking for a way to earn my keep. There was a temp job at Target for a month here, a position to set appointments to sell credit cards machines for two weeks there, and so on. That one was wild, because one of their best employees was a young black guy with the best voice *ever*. Sounded like a young Waylon Jennings, but dressed like he was out of a rap video. The contrast, and his talent, were striking. White people ate it up, in the person, and on the phone. Told them he was 'just a good ol' boy, never meanin' no harm,' and damn did they *love* it. He usually made his weekly quota in a little over two days, and then everything else was gravy money for him the rest of the pay period. Why couldn't *I* do that? People said I had a good voice, was funny, smart, but this position, like every other, never quite seemed to work . . .

And that's what led me here. So embarrassed. So ashamed. Michelle holding me as I cry for the first time in a decade, and having to tell this grown man everything will be okay. She says I can stay with her, use her car while she's at work, so I can find a job, and get back on my feet. I say that I don't deserve her sympathy, nor want her charity, and that she should send me on my way. We've known each other three months, and I literally have nothing in life to offer, nothing going my way. She says that's not true, and that I have an incredible mind, a great sense of humor, a way with words, kind heart, and that I have *her*.

That's a *great* pep talk. Straight out of a Hallmark romance, dog wearing sweater, secret prince revealed, hokey Christmas love story, TV movie of the week territory. And that's what I do—follow her advice to the letter. Got a part-time job at another phone marketing company not long after that speech. I then took a break in the middle of writing this, and got hired on the spot as a GameStop Assistant Manager— which is weird because I haven't played video games in maybe seven years, and didn't know what the manager or those kids in the store were talking about in regards to points, shooter scenarios, team play, online connectivity . . . *Sure*. But I'll make it work. Because I *have* to. And I'll keep putting one foot in front of the other. Because that's the thing to do. I have people that need me. I have the kids, you, Mama Dear, and Michelle. And I have everyone—including myself—that I want to make proud one day.

Merry Christmas, and God Bless.

- Manny

March 9, 2011

I was able to get a police dispatcher job for the City of Carrollton, which is a city in the northern part of DFW. This position came about based on my academy experience as a police recruit. My training supervisor is named Dusty. *Awesome* name. She is extremely intelligent and pleasant, tells the corniest jokes, and is married to an officer (Nicknamed Officer Smiley for his pleasant demeanor. Another excellent name.) for the city. One of the other training supervisors is Brenda. She is whip smart also, a bit blunt, and *loves* Lebron James. Told her I won't hold that against her—but it's all about Kobe.

- Manny

May 6, 2011

I finally found him, Selita, my dad, via his daughter, and it looks like she has had a pretty good life. I am in the process of writing her this letter. It's not a slight to you or Mama Dear at all . . . but I have to reach out. I just have to. This is what I sent.

Hi There. My name is Manny Williams—and I am your brother. All apologies for the title. But I thought I better jump right to the point in case you saw a strange e-mail address and deleted it.

I was born in May of 1979. Your dad—*our* dad—was a manager at a bowling alley in Northwest Houston off of Little York, I think. My mom was nineteen years old and in college at TSU, working part time. That would have made him around twenty-five at the time. My mom's name is Selita.

It's a tale as old as time—he was with your mother, and they were already married. Subsequently, he had an affair, and my mom got pregnant. She naively thought they would be together, and then he went back to your mom, if he had ever left her at all, that is . . .

One reason I heard he did not claim me was besides the whole 'child born out of wedlock' angle was because I was disfigured. My face and head were burned really badly when I was six months old. It looks a little better now, after a ton of reconstructive surgery, but it was quite gruesome when I was a baby. For a while, before y'all switched, he and your family also went to the same church as us, Saint Monica's off of West Montgomery and South Victory in Acres Homes.

I heard my mom started going there in hopes of seeing your dad and maybe getting him to see or acknowledge me. And probably, on some delusional level, she wanted to get your dad to leave your mom and take her back. But he never saw/spoke/called/met/supported me in any way, shape, or form. *At all.* Even though we went to the same church, and my grandmother's house, where I lived my entire childhood, is literally right around the corner from it (less than a half a mile). This had to be where he picked my mom up and dropped her off when they dated, as she lived there as well.

I asked my mom about him a few times, but she was reluctant to talk. All I knew was bits and pieces—his name (she only told me when I pressed her on it when I was twenty), but not the correct spelling. Also, that he was of small build, played on a baseball team for fun, and that I looked just like him—a cause of concern as I grew older and reminded my mother of him more and more by the day.

When I was twenty-two, I looked on the internet and found nothing. I looked again when I was twenty-four, with the same result. Finally, a few days ago, I gave it another try and found a hit—the right general age, right city, and then I found a link online when he was Employee of the Month for HISD in April 2004. When I then saw the pic of him attached, my girlfriend and I were blown away. I have enclosed some pics of me so you can compare. I weigh more than him, but look at the eyes, nose, ears, even the mustache, and I think you can easily see the resemblance.

Again, I apologize and am aware that this is a lot to spring on you, but it is a lot for me as well. I debated whether to contact you at all, but I found the will to do it, and here we are. A little about me: I went to Catholic school—St. Rose of Lima—for the first six years, until my mom lost her job. I graduated from the Engineering Program at Booker T Washington High in 1997. I did pretty well and got a scholarship to the Univ. of Houston where I graduated in May 2001 with a B.S. in political science. I was accepted to a few law schools and went to South Texas College of Law but dropped out. I was working at the same time to help support my mom and siblings, and I just couldn't pull it off.

I have never been arrested, never been to jail, never done drugs, never struck a woman or harmed a child, and I do not smoke or drink. I was an altar boy, a boy scout, won a few science fairs, got humiliated in a few spelling bees, I was vegetarian from age nineteen to twenty-six, stopped for five years, and have picked it back up this year. I have done animal rescue and volunteer work. I played the clarinet in band, play the keyboard, and keep telling myself I will learn the guitar someday. I love basketball, books of all kinds, writing, traveling, and learning about other cultures. And orange Tic Tac's, definitely love me some orange Tic Tac's. Chocolate and soda are my weaknesses.

I worked with law enforcement, and I was actually three-fourths through the police academy before an illness kept me from completing. I have saved a coworker's life before, worked as a nonprofit fundraiser in the education field . . .

I also have a girlfriend of a year and a half, Michelle, who is a teacher in Dallas. I moved here in April 2009, after living my entire life before that in Houston. Michelle is kind, brilliant, traveled the world with her church, plays a few instruments, and speaks several languages—and is *much* better than I deserve. I do not have any kids of my own, but if I did, I would be most honored if she was the mother and we were married . . .

Getting back, I looked for info on our dad having any kids and quickly saw in the Employee of the Month post that he had one daughter, and about an hour or so later, I came across your e-mail address.

Bottom line: Did I have a tough life? Yes. Did I grow up in poverty and face things during the day and night that I would never wish upon my worst enemy? Yeah. Do I wish he had shown just the slightest interest, or at least talked/met me once? You bet. And while I am not a saint or martyr, I am also not vindictive. I am not spiteful and I am not a bad person.

I also am not writing to ask for anything, or to rant and rave, though I'm sure it must seem that way. But I am curious though: Is he God-fearing? Did he ever mention me? And also—what kind of man/ father did you find him to be growing up? And how about now? Was he kind, smart, distant, moody? Does he have other kids out there that you are aware of? Did he treat you well growing up? Is he still with your mother, treat her with respect after the initial affair, and change his ways? Are there any medical conditions on his side of the family that I should be aware of? How was your relationship with your grandparents? Are they both still alive? Did he seem like the kind of man who loved his family above all else and would never turn his back on his own child? And deep, deep down, if you had to make a guess— do you think he ever truly felt sorry for how he treated me, maybe in the way he carried himself, or in a sadness you saw in him from time to time, as if something was weighing on his soul—or do you think he was in fact capable of brushing me off, not thinking twice, and going on about his life as if I never existed?

Those are some of the questions I asked myself a million times growing up—and even up to this very day, in those quiet moments when I tend to look back and reflect. And if you don't think you need to answer them, or to ask him about me, that's quite okay, too. Maybe some things—and some people—should stay out of sight and out of mind . . .

However, I am extremely interested as to what his response would be if you asked him about me. Look in his eyes, because after so many years of living a lie, sometimes people do truly begin to believe it themselves . . .

But regardless of that potential outcome, above all else, I wanted to let you know that I am out here, and I do exist. If you ever want to write or talk and tell me more about you and your life, then that would be great. And if you don't, that would be fine as well. I am not crazy enough to imagine a bond/relationship could or should be formed after all these years—all these decades. But I always felt that a piece of me was missing, a part of my life incomplete, and I prayed to God over and over that it would be brought into the light . . .

Take care, and thank you very much for your time and consideration.

God Bless.

- Manny

❧

May 15, 2011

I reached out again a week or so later, and my sister has finally replied back. She said it was a lot to take in, and is still trying to grasp it all—fair enough. My message was directed at her work e-mail, and that was jarring also—double fair. But in my defense, it was the only one I could find to reach out.

She stated that she did notice a sadness in him, and she had wondered what was behind it over the years. She said we looked *so much* alike . . . She also told me that she studied overseas, learned music, and had a great relationship with him—and that she just did not want to jeopardize that by putting herself in the middle of this . . .

Hers was literally like a bizzaro version of my life. I love all things UK-related—she got to travel and study there. I loved music, but could not afford lessons to get really good outside of band, and tried to teach myself a few instruments, whereas she was a music director. I wished for a father to be there, support me, be proud of me, and love me. Check, check, and check for her. You get the idea. To say that I was extremely jealous of her would be an exercise in brutal honesty.

She suggested I try to reach out to him again—which I already had. Said he had divorced her mom a good while back, moved in with his sister, retired from his job, and was still in Houston. She was recently engaged to be married, or is married, I forget. She empathized with how I grew up, and complimented me on making something of myself, but ultimately suggested my issues with him *were my own* and separate of her—which I already knew . . .

I don't believe in fairy tales, but maybe once every decade or so, I do allow myself to be optimistic. And this one of those exceptions. I thought she might . . . care *more.* But as I did not have any influence over how tough my childhood was, she wasn't the cause of hers being 'ideal.' My mother was the young temptress, hers was the put-upon wife whose husband had the gall to cheat on her with a member of their shared congregation, and had to deal with the embarrassment of the baby coming around to Sunday's service.

Can you really care for someone you've never known? Can you really want to be a part of and interject yourself into the tragic life of someone who could have been you, if not for a twist of fate? Would you want the soul-crushing reminder of the failings in humanity of a man who raised you, treated you well, and was an ideal father for the first three decades of your life?

I think not. And I am not sure if she could see it from the words or tone or essence of what I wrote, but I truly did not want anything from her, or from him for that matter—beyond *acknowledgment.* Not a grab for money, a play for attention, or affection like you see on soap operas, when a long-lost (poor) relation springs out of the woodworks to wreak havoc on the lives of the well-established and well-loved heroes.

I was way beyond back child support, too old for lapsed birthday parties, too uninterested and realistic to believe I would be embraced fully and paraded around their family like a shiny new toy, or prodigal son returned home. She said she would be open to a dialogue, but I didn't really believe her. And even if she did—it would be on her terms, from a distance, curated and bespoke, so as to not interrupt her life with *Him.*

And I know that he definitely was not open to one, or he would have reached out in the last thirty-one or so years—and that was not the case. He went to my church, he knew where my grandmother lived, he met my aunts and cousins, probably saw me on TV when I got my surgery, or read about me in the papers when they published my scholarships and science fair wins. I was *extremely* approachable and easy to find—he was not.

So maybe by getting no answers from him, and limited interest from her, all of my questions were answered in a way. Maybe that chapter is closed and never to be revisited—locked away in a corner of my soul, a story never again to be told. And maybe that's the way it was always meant to be, and was always going to be . . .

- Manny

July 11, 2011

Today's date is 7/11, and it definitely is a lucky set of numbers for me. I have parlayed that dispatcher job to a position with Southwest Airlines, working with their internal help desk, called Source of Support. There is an interesting mix of people and personalities here for sure. Some ridiculously ruthless ones as well, particularly in our immediate department—both line staff and especially the Supervisor's. One really standup guy is Red (a.k.a. Val), who always had my back, and even gave an apartment reference for me *and* a job reference for Michelle, and she has finally gotten hired for her dream job as an English teacher. Really was so kind of him to do, and we appreciate it very much.

Hanging in there one day at a time.

- Manny

April 10, 2013

Janet passed today. She wasn't even sixty-five. Super full of life, smart, loud, heavy on the opinions. She helped me out an *unbelievable* number of times with the kids, with advice, transportation, food . . . Little Greg is, and forever will be, *broken*. They often fought like caged dogs, but loved each other deeply. She was so proud of how smart and kind he is, as she should be . . .

He reached out to tell me via e-mail, and it was the first time I had spoken to him in five years maybe. I had no words of encouragement or strength, just told him how sorry I am for him, and how great a person she was. She took care of Mama Dear so well—grocery store trips, the bank, bills, advice, a shoulder to lean on when everyone else drove her crazy—it really was a template in kindness and patience for me growing up in how to treat others and put them above yourself. And such a burden to bear. I guarantee it shortened her life . . .

Janet used to take me to the Teacher Supply for school supplies and science fair materials. She would type up the report for me because I did not have a computer (or word processor back in the day), and Rosalind helped me with the design of the three-sided backboard—the borders, decoration, placement of the writing. I had no idea Janet was working nights and was using her sleep time during the day to do this. Year after year. Or when she bought me a nice suit in fifth grade and did a write-up for MLK's "I Have a Dream" so I could present it during Black History Month (for a majority crowd of nonblack kids, some of whom told me to my face that my high grade on the presentation was only due to my race). Things that you would not, *could not* do Selita—they had your back. Your mother and your sisters. I was never a child without a parent, even during the times you were checked out. Nah, in fact I had about six of them at various times throughout my life—Mama Dear, Janet, Arleta, Olivia, Rosalind, and Lynell. And Little Greg, Uncle June Bug, Big Greg, D.J., Dreis, and Uncle Eugene stepped in at crucial times as well, during key moments of my life, as supportive father/big-brother-type figures when they could.

And now, one of them is gone, and will be truly missed.

-Manny

August 25, 2013

I have finally achieved a lifelong dream—moving to California. I used that Southwest job as stepping stone to vault Michelle and I into the friendly skies, and get the heck out of Texas. Found a pretty good job get my foot in the door in their university system. It has (once I make it through my probationary period) union protection, good benefits, and a large department with the opportunity to move on to other careers of interest. I found an apartment (rent really is not that bad compared to nice places in Dallas—you want to live big, you pay big, live small, pay small). Having said that, I am sleeping on the floor, as I can't afford furniture yet, and have to wait till we drive our stuff out here. I finally made it to the dentist for the first time in eighteen years or so. Lack of insurance at some points, crippling fear of the dentist at all points . . . My mouth is so bad, but the doctor says he can help me. Super mean, but super good at his job. After just one treatment, my gums feel better. He berates me, asking if I am flossing more regularly. I indicate yes, and he tells me, "Don't lie to me, Mr. Manny. Lie to yourself and fool yourself, but never me!" The *intensity*, I love it.

Michelle's birthday is today, and this cross-country move will be even more tough than normal because my job offer just came through, and her school year back in Texas just started. She is super dedicated, loves her kids and making a difference for the better. She won't join me until Christmas break—so that's four months apart. She is worried I will fall in love with someone else during my alone time there. Told her she's crazy. I would never leave her—unless I somehow ran into Halle Berry or Rihanna at some Caribbean or Southern themed restaurant known to cater to the discerning gentleman *and* gentlelady), and then all bets are *off*.

Will let you know how it turns out. Alone again, naturally.

- Manny

December 30, 2013

Now I will tell you how California is. Work is interesting to say the least. I have a graveyard shift job. It's going nowhere, but it is easy. Therefore, I decided to double down and get a day job at a hospital as well doing admin work. I now work the night job Thursday through Sunday, from 8 p.m. to 6:30 a.m. Then the day job is Monday through Friday, from 8 a.m. to 4:30 p.m. I mostly sleep on Saturday and Sunday mornings and afternoons, and that's about it.

This is definitely 'no country for old men' . . . But I am making decent money to pay the bills out here, saving a little. Have paid down on both of our credit cards, and made a tiny dent in our student loans (yes, I know I am too old to still have them), and am stashing some away for the future. Got my first new car ever, a base model Camaro with a racing stripe—yes, I am *that* guy. Told Michelle she's *lucky* I didn't go for a used Vette.

Michelle made it up two weeks ago. She *loves* it. Except the weird stuff. People bike on the streets—including the freeway . . . umm yeah. They refuse to use the sidewalks. Electric cars are everywhere, and I had never saw one before moving here. They are super quiet and sneaky. And ridiculously slow. Fun fact—I failed my driving test the first time out here. Definitely underestimated it, and they have some tricky rules I had never heard of. No fast-food places within a five-mile radius of my job. And there are only like two gas stations nearby. Guess it's a bit unseemly for the rich crowd I work near . . .

Michelle was able to land a new teaching job already. Insane. Drove her around and put in resumes everywhere for all the high schools, in all the neighboring cities, within a forty-five-minute radius from our apartment. I didn't even think you could do that stuff post 9/11, but they let her walk in and drop off resumes, and, in some instances, she even got pre-interviews with principals on the spot.

So far so good. Really missed her, and I'm glad to be together again. Will let you know how things keep going. Until then.

- Manny

January 11, 2014

First Janet, and now this—Mama Dear passed away today. The feelings are overwhelming. I have always loved her deeply, but due to our situation and how she expected me to care for you and the kids, my feelings evolved to include a revolving wheel of anger, sadness, despair, and ultimately resignation to my fate.

She loved everyone, looked out for them, raised her children, raised her children's children. Loved the Lord and her husband with every inch of her soul—even though they both seemingly withheld their love in return many-a-time . . .

I never told you this, but I went to Houston with Michelle in late July 2013, and was able to see Mama Dear one last time. She was suffering from dementia by then and was not all the way there. But, for a moment, maybe a few moments, I saw her eyes light up, and she seemed to remember me a bit. Michelle was moved to tears and was honored that she could meet the woman who raised me, and who I hold in such regard.

We drove by Mama's house. Michelle grew up lower middle-class outside of Waco, and thought she knew going without, and being raised on a check-to-check existence, she really didn't know until she saw our neighborhood firsthand what *true poverty* was. I told her it was a different kind of life, but the only one I knew. I was not embarrassed. Or maybe I was, and still am . . .

I didn't want to tell you or the kids, because I had nothing to say. Nothing mean, nothing kind, nothing inspirational. It has been so long—what, three or four years since we spoke in person? I literally don't have a single thing give or offer. I didn't make it big in Dallas, didn't become a police officer, didn't get my head right, or lose weight, or learn to love myself and others better.

All I got was peace of mind. Quiet. Wrapped in shame, and a feeling of knowing that I walked away from everyone and everything, because I had to, or I would have died in that city. I was pulled in every direction, asked to do everything, expected to have all the answers. But I am not the hero of my own story, or anyone else's for that matter. 'Fake it till you make it' only goes so far—and when you *don't* make it, the nervous breakdown comes. Followed by losing/quitting the job, followed by putting on seventy-five pounds from eating away the feelings, and too many dates to count, desperate to find someone to lie and say you are worthy of love when you know clearly, and quite contrarily, that you are not. I was, and still am ashamed of how I left. But I am also happier—and angry at myself for not doing it *much sooner*.

What if I went to New York or LA for college? What if I met that rep from Dartmouth who had a near full ride, and made a special request to my counselor to meet me at college day? What if I never used that lawsuit money for my head on you and the kids, went to Junior College, saved the difference on my scholarships and grants, took out the max amount in federal loans, and disappeared to Cali to be a writer or an actor. What if I stumbled across someone else running away from home at an earlier age who could love me and change me for the better? And I didn't have my guard up, insecurities galore, and was receptive to that love?

Or on the other side, what if I went out there and lost all that money, was robbed and beaten, to die alone in a ditch? I will never know. And not knowing hurts *immensely*. Was my life and all its choices predetermined by poverty and circumstance? Could I have fought all those beasts on my own without you and the kids to *weigh me down*? Or, were you my convenient *crutches* used to prop myself up, and use as an excuse to explain away my lack of bravery and initiative?

I gave up so many years for you all, and I have *nothing* to show for it. I just learned that Dante was in jail again. Jamon is also still locked up, Stephanie took off to Louisiana with God knows who. Greg is alone, Dominique is a mother, Cheyenne has your face, you are still sick, and Mama Dear is still dead. I did nothing. I accomplished nothing. I am *nothing*.

- Manny

P.S. Mama Dear would have turned eighty-nine in exactly two more weeks, but she didn't need another second in this world, because she already had her crown waiting on her in heaven—all she had to do was pick it out once she gets there . . .

*May 11, 2014*

*This is going to be the last letter I ever send to you, Selita—but in many ways, it will also be my first . . . This is on paper because I'm in my car writing in my notebook. It's dark, and I'm hoping I don't run down the battery using this little center console light. I just can't be in the house right now. I don't want to have Michelle see me weak, and afraid, and crying over a letter and a life's worth of memories.*

*Anyway, the reason I am going to stop writing is because I finally realize that your story, our is never going to end. We just keep going in circles, for decades on end, and I'm so tired of it. We fight and make up. Make up and fight. I forgive you and then you turn on me again. I lash out from some pent-up aspersion from a lifetime ago, and then I go too far and hurt your feelings. I send you to the hospital and you come away worse than ever—proving your theory that you were right and did not belong there. Could I ever stop being that scared little boy? Would I? . . .*

*Too many of these stories need to stay in the dark where they belong—and would have remained if not for my misguided intentions. And now I hear through the grapevine that you are threatening to move to Louisiana, or some other random state (with a real and/or imaginary boyfriend) that I have never heard of before, and try to make the kids go along with you?*

*Are you insane?! I mean, mentally ill I get, but I am speaking of true insanity here. There is no way I would ever allow that . . . But then I realize, I have no say. Stephanie is twenty-seven now, Dominique is twenty-three, Dante is twenty-two, and Cheyenne is twenty-one. They aren't 'kids' anymore—they are adults. And I have no say over them, or you . . . And never really did.*

*I am now seven hours into that twenty-one-hour drive home to Houston. I am going to leave Michelle. Tell her my family needs me, how I never should have left Texas for California, and that she's the right person at the wrong time, with the wrong partner. And then lie to her that maybe, just maybe, when this pain ends, I know I'm going to see her again . . .*

*The only reason I never went ahead and adopted them after all those years was the slimmest of hopes that you might get your sense back. So that you could see I was never against you after all, and was merely acting as a placeholder of sorts until you got better and could be a true part of the family again. But no matter what I have done, sacrificed, bought, stole, or borrowed to keep us together, you never once even pretended to care. Paying bills, getting the kids through school, and two into college (at least temporarily)—homes in nice neighborhoods others would die for. None of it mattered to you . . .*

*Who else would bust his butt to do that for a woman he's not even sure he likes on a day-to-day basis?! But hey, you know what they say about, "Stone walls do not a prison make, nor iron bars a cage." And in spite of my best intentions, it seems I have constructed a prison for us all . . .*

*And I suppose that's what you imagine me doing to you, right? All these years, keeping you locked up. Your son is really your warden, my acts of kindness acts are torture, your children are your fellow convicts, forced to suffer under my cruel watch. Well, no more.*

*I am about halfway there now. Flying down I-5, begging one of these highway cops to chase me, hoping for a rock or a tire to creep up on my wheels in the darkness, causing a blowout in the dark, and send me careening toward . . . death . . . Life? Nothingness? . . .*

*But that will not happen now, because for once in my life, I have true clarity—and I am going to turn this car around. I will, in fact, not be letting Michelle go, and mortgaging my future. I will instead choose to shed my past. Lose my baggage. Release my chains. Free my soul. By letting you, Houston, the kids, the memories, and the pain go, once and for all.*

*That it's comes to this is shocking. The realization that the lady who brought me life as a single parent, that I felt so bad for, because I burdened her life with my surgeries and scars, shortcomings and short stature—is probably better off without me. Oh, how protective of you I was as a small boy—never knowing the hurt and pain we would inflict on each other in the name of . . . I don't even know.*

*But now I'm through, Selita. I'm past it all—the guilt, the anger, the everything. I'm going to leave this Exxon rest stop where I've pulled over and head back toward where I truly belong now, on a path all my own. And though I wish I could say that this will help us keep the peace—being in different parts of the country—I know that would be a wasted wish. My hope is that this separation by distance will mean that we'll never fight over money anymore, or what's best for the kids (young adults) that we basically shared custody of all these years. But, of course, we'll fight. And then, time will pass, and something will bring us back together: The birth of a child, the passing of an family member, a breakdown, or hospitalization. And we'll put our game faces on and be civil and somewhat friendly for the prying eyes—praying there will be actual remnants of love as opposed to disdain.*

*I got your new address from Little Greg when I came down to visit Mama Dear. I drove by hoping to catch a glimpse of you or Dominique (Greg said that you lived with her and her boyfriend and child), and lo and behold, there you were. The shades, the scarf, standing, well, pacing, at a bus stop. Smiling. Talking to the radio (and yourself) while laughing. You always were your own best company. You weren't 'cured' or 'healed' or whatever medical new age term people use when discussing mental illness. I noticed that instantly. But what I noticed even more, was how you no longer needed me. It had been years since I had seen you in person, and you were okay. The world kept on spinning, life moved on, and so did you. Without me hovering, or hollering or hoping. You lived your life, as you had before I entered, as you have since I exited. It should have been apparent that you didn't need me, and even more importantly, the fact that I no longer needed you . . .*

*Yet although we don't need each other, that does not change the fact that we were meant for each other. I'll eventually settle down in my career, perhaps marry Michelle, and maybe, just maybe have children of my own. But you will always be just around the corner, not in my presence, but always in my thoughts.*

*I have made way back home now, and am sneaking in. Well, that's not true. Michelle sleeps like the dead and snores like a grizzly bear, so no need to sneak at all. Just one more reason that I love her. She has a soul that bends, but will not break, and I see the pain in her eyes that belies her age. Is that a recipe for disaster, two wounded souls flying together in the night? Ah, wouldn't be my first mistake, but it could be my best. And with that, I have decided that I will marry Michelle one day. It's just that simple. She is a good person. And I think with her close by, maybe I could be a good person, too . . . Don't know when, or how I'll pay for a ring or a honeymoon or if it will last. But I want to make it last. And I want to keep her near. And to have something good in my life, for once, and forever, that is all my own . . .*

*I know I've messed up. Quit good jobs and dropped out of law school (twice), showed cruelty to those who loved me, chased affection from those who barely tolerated me, used you and the children as a totem, an anchor, a "Get into Heaven free" card at various times, often within the same day . . .*

*Regardless, I always stormed out that front door each morning to conquer the world and slay all demons, but never for myself. For y'all. It's always been for y'all. Nobody else really needs me the way you and the kids did, and I'd be telling a humongous lie if I tried to deny that kept me sticking around way longer than I intended.*

*And come to think of it, I should actually be lying right now. Drawing myself as more selfless, and noble, and anything Tom Cruise might paint himself as in a movie where he's wearing a crisp white shirt (he looks great in white) and running superfast to-and-fro, saving the day.*

*So much of the time I sit up, wondering if you woke up one day and were no longer sick, where our lives would we be. Would we still have nightmares of past pains? Would there be future ones, even worse, left to see? . . .*

*But that day will most likely never come. The perfect time, the pristine moment, the opportunity for tears and laughter, and old grievances forgiven, and new promises forged. So, instead, I will say those things* now—and not let another moment pass with these words beating and swirling around in my chest. Man, I wish I could write as fast as I can feel . . . Because I've never been so honest with myself, let alone with you. Call me delusional, but I truly believe that somehow, someway, we will both eventually, be okay.

Listen Selita, no, scratch that. I'm will stop calling you that because it's too familiar and it's a backhanded way of lessening who you are—and what you mean to me. Because if I say Ma—if I call you that magic word, it opens the door to allowing you to matter. Allowing you to walk back into my heart. Allowing you to run back into my soul . . .

Listen Mama, there's something I need to say . . . Through it all— and I mean it all—the poverty, the hurtful words, the broken hearts, the loneliness, the lying and stealing, the mental hospitals, abusive boyfriends, the fights, the fear, the paranoia, the surgeries, the threats, the shame and the blame, you treating me bad, and me using it as both an excuse to treat you worse, times when I still believed in God, but often questioned whether he believed in me . . . Mama, I need you to hear that you are not alone. I will always be there for you, and I have never stopped loving you.

And even if, unimaginably, you've somehow yet to reach your worst, or me mine, that is something that will forever remain the same. This guarantee is eternal, from your son by both fate, as well as by choice.

With all the love that God will allow me to summon, and then a little bit more after that, I want to wish you a Happy Mother's Day, and ask that you please tell those kids that I love them with all my heart.

- Manny

P.S. For the first time, Mama, my soul will rest in peace. Hopeful, because it seems that you could be what you once were, and might forever remain— happy—in more than just my dreams . . .

*May 24, 2014*

*This came in the mail a few days ago, but I have yet to open it up, scared as to what I might find inside . . . I'm guessing the UPS store in Dallas forwarded it to the one in Cali. Nice of them considering I haven't paid them in a year or so. I know some people in the family have been searching for me. Hunting me down like a fugitive. And from second hand accounts I just barely missed running into them in Dallas, at my old job, and even my apartment complex. I just need time on my own. And when ready, I'll reach out, I promise . . .*

*This is the first letter I can ever recall you sending me in my life. After all the hundreds that I've written to you, via paper, email, Sanskrit markings on the wall, not once did you reply back until now. Thank you. Today is my 35ᵗʰ birthday, and I have so much on my mind. So many thoughts, memories, nightmares. This means a lot to me. More thank you can ever know. You must have been on the right mix of medicine, or been in a good frame of mind, or something. Because you sound . . . good. And in a proper frame of mind. And not sick. Not sure if this is a fluke day, or the quiet before the storm. But I will gladly take it.*

*It went as follows:*

*Dear Mr. Williams:*
*I hope this letter finds you well.*

*I discovered a lot of your documents and have been keeping them for you upon your return. But it has been many years now and I doubt you will ever come back at this point. Your siblings both miss you and are extremely mad at you for leaving. I have repeatedly informed them that this is unfair. You had no* responsibilities to them or to me and you stayed much longer to help us than anyone could have expected of you.

I came across an old picture of you walking to the school bus, and remembered how funny it was that you always walked with your head down, like a sad puppy dog. But then I felt it was more like you were scared to look up, and make direct eye contact with people. So they can't see you, seeing them, as they watch and stare at you and your scars. Or maybe more so that you are unsure of where you are stepping, and if you were to walk in the wrong spot, as if the earth might open up and swallow you whole.

Always scared. Always waiting for the next bad thing to happen. And that is my fault, I suppose. I raised you to be scared, and placed all of you in scary situations. Please know it was not on purpose. My thoughts and my mind get away from me from time to time, as you are well aware. I tried my best. And I thank you, because I know you tried your best too. Please do not worry about coming back, as we will be ok. And so will you.

Happy Birthday to My Oldest Son.

God bless your kind heart, Manny Williams.

Love,
Mama Selita

CPSIA information can be obtained
at www.ICGtesting.com
Printed in the USA
LVHW021657160622
721463LV00002B/264

9 780578 730172